QUILT ME!

JANE BROCKET

QUILT ME!

Using inspirational fabrics to create
over 20 beautiful quilts

COLLINS & BROWN

First published in the United Kingdom in 2014 by
Collins & Brown
10 Southcombe Street
London
W14 0RA

An imprint of Anova Books Company Ltd

Distributed in the United States and Canada by
Sterling Publishing Co, 387 Park Avenue South, New York,
NY 10016-8810, USA

ISBN 978-1-90844-925-2

A CIP catalogue record for this book is available from the
British Library.

10 9 8 7 6 5 4 3 2 1

Photography by Catherine Gratwicke
Illustrations by Sam Brewster

Reproduction by Rival Colour, UK
Printed by 1010 Printing International Ltd, China

This book can be ordered direct from the publisher
at www.anovabooks.com

FOR ALICE

CONTENTS

INTRODUCTION

One of the most exciting ways to start a quilt is with fabric inspiration. For me, this happens when I come across a fabric that is so lovely/ cleverly designed/unusual/colourful/meaningful that I want to create a quilt around it, to show it off, to see it and use it. It is this approach that is the focus of this book; every quilt here has sprung directly from a type or design of fabric that has shouted, 'Quilt Me!' very loudly and very clearly.

We have at our disposal a wealth of wonderful fabrics for making quilts. In recent years, much patchwork and quilting has focused on shop-bought, purpose-made, lightweight quilting cottons: I'm not saying that these aren't fabulous, but I am saying that there is a whole new world of alternative textiles to be discovered by the adventurous quilter who wants to create unique, individual, unusual and beautiful quilts. To use these fabrics is not so much a radical departure as a welcome return to the approach that thrifty, resourceful, inventive patchworkers have always applied when seeking out and making the most of the vast range of available fabrics. It's also a return to traditional patchwork and quilting values; to the idea of using whatever is to hand, whether it's a furnishing fabric, an old garment or a practical household textile.

In this book, my personal quilting philosophy and approach remain exactly the same as in my first quilt book, *The Gentle Art of Quilt-Making*: start with lovely fabrics, choose simple shapes and designs, don't worry about perfection, throw out unnecessary rules and complications, and enjoy making and using quilts. I continue with the liberated, joyous, colourful approach that I enjoy so much, and offer designs and ideas for quilts to be made in a non-competitive, have-a-go, gentle, simple way – but this time with all sorts of different fabrics.

I have always loved fabrics – ever since I was little, when my favourites were the felt squares I bought at the market, and the tiny amounts of velvet in the empty jewellery boxes I was allowed to keep. With time, my wishlist of fabrics has grown, and I still enjoy shopping and looking for fabrics as much as ever. There is enormous pleasure to be had in the process, in the searching, rummaging, rescuing, discovering and uncovering. It is tremendously exciting to come across something that makes your hands itch to cut out and quilt, to be inspired by a wonderful colour scheme, design or pattern. It is also gratifying to make the most of what can be found in our homes and in our traditional fabric shops, to explore our very rich textile heritage, and to consider alternatives to quilting cottons, such as clothes, curtains, upholstery, tablecloths and interior decoration. The quilts shown here are made from fabrics I have found in many different places, although I still harbour dreams of the perfect one-stop shop that I could walk into and find all the textiles I treasure: ticking, linen, vintage, gingham, hand-embroidered, indigo, tweed, tartan, suiting, shirting, velvet, silk and calico, and more.

Having done my fair share of fabric-hunting, I would always say that if you find a fabric that shouts 'quilt me!' at you, do answer the call. Whether it's fabric

on a roll or a used, vintage, second-hand garment or tablecloth or curtain, I advise you to swoop when you see something good or unusual, as it may not be there another time. When buying by the length, it's always worth investing in as long a piece as you can afford, but a metre or half-metre of anything you really love will be enough to act as a catalyst for a quilt. Plus, it's always possible to supplement a rare/vintage/fine fabric with other fabrics; this is where quilting cottons are so useful, as they are brilliant for mixing in. Indeed, unusual fabric combinations are fascinating and can produce lovely effects; your entire quilt does not have to be made from silk or tweed, and a mix can make a highlight fabric look even more striking.

Please do not feel confined to, or restricted by, the fabrics I have used here; the great thing about the 'quilt me!' approach is that so many fabrics can be used. The quilts shown are made with what I have been able to find so far, but I know that there are many more amazing fabrics waiting to be quilted. It's worth keeping an open mind as to the possibilities of what can be included; just think how previous generations used what they could get hold of and were actually far less rule-bound and quilting-cotton-bound than we are today. Take lessons and inspiration from them; from the quilters of Gee's Bend who knew and still know how to improvise, and how to bend and break the rules (but who ever said those rules were the right rules?), and from any quilters whose quilts you like and who follow their instincts and personal taste in fabric.

These 'quilt me!' quilts are a way of weaving our rich textile heritage into our quilted creations, and of preserving something of that heritage. As fewer people make their own clothes and soft furnishings, many fabric manufacturers and shops struggle to survive. It would be terrible if we lost more historic and beautiful fabrics (some have already all but disappeared), and those that do survive need to be memorialised, even if it's only by means of little scraps and pieces in quilts, which then add up to wonderful textile texts. Using many different fabrics is a way of adding excitement, texture, interest, history and significant design to our quilts. It's also a way of recognising, preserving and continuing our valuable textile history.

Jane Brocket

INSPIRATIONAL FABRICS

The following is a directory of the different fabrics used in this book, but it is by no means an exhaustive list of all the fabric and textile possibilities available to the curious and adventurous quilter. I give a short overview of each fabric and indicate the merits and/or difficulties of working with it.

When choosing a fabric for quilt-making, avoid anything that is very loose-weave or very open-weave, as it will fray and distort very quickly. Avoid stretchy fabric (anything knitted or containing Lycra), as it will lose its shape. Any fabric with pleats or a surface texture (for example, some seersuckers) that could be lost after cutting or during ironing is best not used. And anything that is very silky/slippery, thin, delicate or lacy is either not robust enough and/or is unsuitable.

COMBINING FABRICS

The general consensus in quilting circles is that you should use fabrics of the same or similar weight in a quilt. This makes practical sense as it ensures the seams are balanced, that quilting either by machine or by hand is straightforward, and that the overall look and feel is harmonious.

However, there is no reason why you shouldn't mix up fabrics as much as you like, providing it's easy to stitch them together. There is no hard-and-fast rule that says you can't put tweed and silk together, or denim and lawn, or corduroy and cotton. In fact, unexpected and original mixes of fabric can create wonderful effects and textures.

The only drawback is the issue of cleaning; as soon as you bring in a fabric such as silk, wool or tweed, you are committing to dry-cleaning your quilt. If this is a problem, keep to washable fabrics only – you will still be able to introduce a wide range of fabrics. Be experimental, take risks, and do something different.

NOTES ON CUTTING AND HANDLING

Many fabrics other than purpose-made quilting cottons can be – to varying degrees – slippery, stretchy, or likely to fray, attributes that can sometimes cause problems with cutting and sewing.

❖ Fabrics with a loose or open weave (for example, tweed or gauze) will relax (and even stretch a little) as soon as they are cut, or as you feed them under the needle, so these need to be handled as little as possible and with extra care. I tend to use these fabrics in squares, strips and rectangles, as anything with points such as triangles or diamonds can fray or distort.

❖ Corduroy also stretches because the flat 'furrows' open up a little horizontally (across the wales, or ridges) once the fabric is cut into small pieces. Take care when cutting and allow for the fact that pieces may become a little larger across the width (but not vertically along the length of the furrows and wales) after cutting.

❖ When cutting, you may find that wool, cord, linen and velvet fabrics move under the ruler. You need to be ready to gently ease the fabric into a straight line along the edge of the ruler, and avoid cutting more than a couple of thicknesses at a time, or you may find that the pressure of your hand on the ruler causes the fabric to slip as you cut and you end up with a wonky or rippled edge.

❖ It helps enormously if you pin the pieces of these trickier fabrics right side together before or as you sew to keep them in place. If it's a really thick, open fabric such as Harris tweed (see page 15), go back and forth at the beginning and end of a seam, just to be sure the pieces are held together securely.

❖ If there are problems with fraying due to an open weave, it may help to use a ½in (1cm) seam allowance when cutting. But do remember to do this with ALL the other fabrics in the quilt top.

❖ Alternatively, cut out fray-prone fabrics with pinking shears or use a pinking blade on your rotary cutter.

❖ Smooth, shiny and delicate fabrics need careful handling to ensure they are cut and sewn accurately. A very smooth fabric (such as silk, lawn, poplin or shirting) does not have enough loose surface fibres to enable it to 'stick' to other layers of the same fabric (quilting cottons 'stick' together well), so cutting more than one thickness at a time can be a little difficult as the layers of fabric move easily under the ruler. In addition, sewing one or more smooth fabrics together requires concentration to ensure that the edges are lined up, and the fabric doesn't slip during sewing. Pinning before sewing helps, as does taking things slowly, not rushing, or working on automatic pilot.

❖ While some fabrics cause problems with too much movement and give, others (such as twill, canvas or silk) are so fine and/or tightly woven that they have no 'give' or stretch at all. These need to be cut as accurately as possible to ensure all seam allowances are correct, as you won't be able to ease (or gently stretch) the fabric later when sewing.

CHOOSING AND BUYING FABRIC

Deciding which fabrics to buy is best done when you have time to browse, consider, reconsider, build up piles of bolts of cloth and play with different combinations. This is the beauty of browsing on the web: it's very easy to fill a shopping basket, take a break and come back to review your selection. It's not always as easy in a busy shop. Don't rush and don't feel you need to rush; these places are used to customers making thoughtful, time-consuming purchases (and if you do feel uncomfortable, then shame on the shop). It's worth asking for a second opinion, too; fabric shop staff can be very helpful and enthusiastic and able to make excellent suggestions.

I rarely decide to buy all the fabric I need for a quilt in one shopping expedition. I discovered early on that it was too easy to get carried away with a theme and the convenience of a single-stop shopping trip, and too often I came home with fabrics that seemed like a good idea in the shop but that I really wished I hadn't bought. If you are going fabric shopping, it's always worth checking what you have at home before you set off so you have a more informed idea of what you actually need. But if you happen to come across a wonderful fabric unexpectedly, buy it; it pays to purchase fewer in terms of numbers of fabrics and more in terms of a fabric you adore. Once you have an amazing starting-point fabric you can take your time, shop around, and buy the rest of the fabrics over time. Your quilt will be all the better for a little extra consideration.

The best way to make good, true decisions is to go browsing when you are looking for nothing in particular and are not under pressure. This is when the fabrics you truly love catch your eye, and you know immediately that you want to make a quilt with them. It's also the time to trust your instincts; I regret very few impulse purchases of stunning fabrics I have found when not looking for anything specific, because I have bought them for all the right reasons and subsequently loved using them.

You may prefer to build up a collection in the traditional thrifty manner, by saving old clothes and household linens, or by cutting up summer dresses and cotton shirts, or by swapping with friends and fellow quilters. But if you are new to quilting, or don't have the resources of used or shared fabrics, or simply prefer to buy new fabric for your quilts, you need some shopping strategies.

❖ The best places to shop are those that offer a good range of fabrics and plenty of inspiration. This may sound obvious, but it's not always that simple. Unless you are able to get to one of the enormous US-style shops that stock a huge number of fabrics, you are limited to the selection made by the owner of a small shop. There are thousands of designs available at any one time, so editing is necessary; if you can find a place where the edited selection matches your tastes, you are in luck. If not, keep trying new places, no matter how apparently unpromising. Or go to one of the major quilt shows and festivals, where there are a number of vendors and plenty of choice.

❖ If you don't have any inspirational fabric shops near you (and there is a woeful lack in the UK), the next best option is to buy online. Looking at photographs of fabric is never the same as seeing and handling the real thing, and there is always an element of risk with colour reproduction and scale of pattern, but the best online sellers offer fantastic choice and excellent service.

❖ When shopping on the web, it's best to play with wishlists and design boards and browse extensively before committing to buy. Put lots of fabrics in the basket but leave them there for a day or two before coming back and being ruthlessly selective.

❖ Before buying, it is worth having a look at your collection to remind yourself of what you have already and what you need. If there's a particular quilt in a book or a fabric design that has inspired you, take the book or the fabric to the shop, or keep your source of inspiration next to the computer for easy reference.

❖ If there's a colour combination you like, take pages from magazines or paint charts to remind you of the exact colours. Unless you have an amazing memory, it's very easy to recall incorrectly and plump for the wrong shade.

FABRIC DIRECTORY

Here is an overview of the various different fabrics I have used in this book, together with some notes on using them.

Quilting cotton

There are many good reasons why lightweight cotton quilting fabrics, designed and sold as such, are ideal for making quilts. They are durable, hardwearing, colourfast, washable and easy to iron. They have an equal number of threads to the warp and weft, which means they do not distort easily, and they keep their shape after cutting. They have a medium-density weave; if they had a more open, loose weave, they would stretch or fray very easily, and if they had a much tighter weave, they would not have the necessary give that allows quilters to 'ease' the fabrics where necessary when sewing and ironing. Quilting cotton is not super-smooth like poplin, lawn or many shirt fabrics, but instead has some short fibres on the surface. This means that layers of the fabric 'stick' together rather than slipping, and this removes the need for pinning. This fabric is also soft to the touch, and wears beautifully.

In addition to the physical properties of light quilting cottons, there are of course aesthetic considerations, and this is where these fabrics really come into their own. Quilting cottons are big business, especially in the US, and there are fabrics to suit every taste. Many fabrics are brilliantly inspirational and can spark off all kinds of ideas for quilts. Increasingly, manufacturers are enlisting the services of talented designers whose name helps to sell the fabrics (see the Lotta Jansdotter fabrics on page 26).

These cotton fabrics make quilting easy because, even if you prefer to sew with only simple shapes, there is no reason why you can't produce a fantastic quilt using clever fabrics designed by someone who knows exactly what they are doing.

Quilting cottons are easy to find if you are willing to use the web for shopping, but do be careful with colour matching. It's still worth seeing a fabric before buying whenever possible, but I know that it's often not.

Shirting and dress fabrics

Any lightweight printed, yarn-dyed or colour-woven cotton fabric is ideal for making quilts. Dresses and skirts cut up beautifully, as do cotton pyjamas, dressing gowns and shirts. High-quality cotton shirts can sometimes be a little too smooth and fine, which makes them tricky to handle, but this isn't a problem when you are using smaller pieces. However, if you use full-width (60in/150cm) shirting off a roll for backing quilts, its smooth surface means it doesn't cling or stick at all to the wadding (even wadding with scrim – see page 142); it simply falls away from it, unlike quilting cottons and many simple dress cottons. The only solution is to use large numbers of pins when making the quilt 'sandwich', or to baste before quilting.

Cotton lawn

Many quilters love Liberty Tana Lawn fabrics. These are very smooth, light, printed cottons, many of which feature the distinctive 'Liberty print' and Arts & Crafts designs. I have tried using a few small pieces in my quilts because the designs are wonderful, but find the fabric is too light and fine for my liking, and it tends to slip when sewing. I'm also not keen on the fact that these fabrics crease easily, and worry that as they are so fine they will be less durable in the long term.

Double gauze cotton

Double gauze isn't particularly well-known, but it is being used by a few – mainly Japanese – designers and companies to create very soft, bouncy, floaty fabrics.

Cotton gauze is a type of muslin (the kind of thing used for bandages and for straining cheese and jam), and has a very open weave. In a single layer it would be totally unsuitable for quilts, but double gauze is created by weaving two layers together. This entails picking up threads to hold the two layers together, which is why there are tiny dots over the surface of the fabric.

Since there are two very airy layers, it is difficult to get double gauze to lie absolutely flat; this means it can be hard to cut out and to piece accurately. The edges also tend to fray and it's possible to lose the seam allowance alarmingly quickly once you start handling the fabric. But it has a lovely drape and handle, and in quilts it feels as though it's already been washed many times. Either use a ½in (1cm) seam allowance, or cut and handle the fabric as little as possible. I imagine it's difficult to machine-quilt double gauze as the fabric would bunch up very quickly, so I recommend hand-quilting with quite long, not-too-tight stitches that don't pucker the surface.

This fabric is not cheap (the result of the production method) and some examples can be narrower than standard quilting cottons. Plus, many of the designs are large-scale, so it's best to use a piece whole in a modern design with a few supplementary fabrics (see the Watercolour quilt on page 40).

Indigo cotton

Authentic indigo fabrics are often piece- or thread-dyed by hand (using a plant-derived dye). Usually it's a simple light- or medium-weight cotton, like a basic tablecloth or hardwearing dress fabric; it is ideal for quilts, although generally speaking it is not very wide.

Be careful if you have real indigo fabric as the dye might run when washed. Pre-wash it, especially if you are planning to mix it with other fabrics. Alternatively, buy the more commercial (and less costly) quilting fabrics that mimic 'real' indigo fabrics.

These cottons are lovely, easy to use, and show up the stitching beautifully (see the Indigo Bento Box quilt on page 106). They fall into the category of being useful and beautiful, not too fine, and absolutely right for quilting.

Barkcloth

Real, traditional barkcloth is a non-woven fabric made from the bark of certain trees in Asia, Africa, Indonesia and the Pacific. However, these days, barkcloth is more commonly associated with a soft, thick, woven cotton fabric with a textured surface that resembles tree bark. It was particularly popular in the post-war years and up to the 1970s, when it was widely used as a furnishing and upholstery fabric. In the UK, it is associated with the 'atomic' 1950s patterns that were popular at the time of the Festival of Britain. In the US, it enjoyed great popularity with lush, large-scale tropical designs in rich, deep colours – the kind of thing you'd see in Elvis Presley films or in bars with rattan furniture. Even today, the best barkcloth designs can be found in the US in vintage fabric stores, and especially in Hawaii.

Barkcloth is usually made from cotton, although some examples might contain a proportion of viscose or linen. It's very washable and durable and, although it is a little thicker than most quilting cottons, it works brilliantly in quilts, bringing wonderful texture and some rare and unusual patterns.

Barkcloth all but disappeared after the 1970s, but the recent explosion of interest in mid-century design has rekindled its popularity, especially among fabric collectors who realise that many of these fabrics feature outstanding, time-specific designs by well-known designers. It's not always easy to go looking for barkcloth; it's more a matter of buying it if you find a piece you like. It is sold by specialist vintage fabric sellers, but lengths (often as curtains) can be found in car boot sales, vintage fairs and flea markets. Any piece of barkcloth in decent condition would make a marvellous starting point for a quilt (see the Wisteria quilt on page 82). It is also (usually) washable, and is very easy to handle.

Vintage hand-embroidered textiles

After years of being hidden away in attics and cupboards, vintage hand-embroidered textiles are enjoying a period of enthusiastic rediscovery by a generation of stitchers and proponents of vintage style, who appreciate the designs, skill and colour choices that went into their making.

As most examples are worked on hardwearing cotton or cotton/linen mix, and the weave of the fabric is even, they are easy to handle, iron, cut up and sew. They are a gift to any quilter who can get over their reluctance to cut into a hand-stitched piece (not always easy, I know). If you really can't take the scissors to a pretty tablecloth, look for examples that may have good areas of stitching but are torn or stained in other parts. Then cut out the good bits, including areas without embroidery that could be useful for borders or plain sections.

Note that some vintage embroideries are on woven viscose fabric, which is very difficult to work with. Although I have bought some on eBay by mistake (some sellers don't mention or don't realise that the fabric is viscose), I have always decided against using them as it's extremely difficult to keep the edges straight and neatly lined up; viscose is slippery and has so much movement in it that the cut-out pieces distort quickly. If you do want to use viscose, it would be a good idea to apply some sort of fabric stiffener; maybe starch or an iron-on backing gauze (the sort you use for machine embroidery).

Métis

Métis is not particularly well known outside a small côterie of vintage French linen enthusiasts and collectors who prize its fine, hardwearing qualities. Métis is a linen union fabric (a linen and cotton mix) that was produced in France for sheeting and tablecloths. The mix of linen and cotton varies, and depends on the date of production since the process was changed in the 1930s; generally speaking it can be 50/50, 70/30 or 30/70. It is usually unbleached or ecru, and is available as ready-hemmed sheets or by the metre (it is often much wider than standard fabrics). Métis comes in various weights, some of which are too heavy and tough for quilting; it helps to have a feel before buying, or to buy from a reputable seller who can advise you.

Métis is a beautiful, tightly woven fabric with a classic, traditional surface texture. You may need to soften métis before using it by giving it a hot wash. The generous widths also mean it is great for backing a quilt (see the Kitchen Sink quilt on page 94). It looks wonderful with other plain, traditional linen and cotton household and practical fabrics, and is very easy to sew with, although it can distort a little along the edges as you cut. It is down-to-earth stuff, and will give years of service in a quilt.

Vintage métis can be bought as sheets or by the metre and is available from specialist French textile dealers, brocantes and on eBay.

Woven woollen fabrics

For quilts, the best woven wool fabric is medium-weight and not too fine and luxurious – partly because of the cost, but also because really good-quality wool fabric can be smooth and difficult to handle. Choose something that is not too thick or loosely woven so that you don't get bulky seams or problems with fraying.

It is a fact of life that quilts containing any proportion of wool fabric should be dry-cleaned only. If you can't face that, it is best to avoid using wool.

Wool checks

There are some excellent medium-weight woven wool or wool and cashmere check fabrics that look lovely in quilts and are easy to handle. Soft wool checks in muted and natural palettes are a great starting point for a quilt, rather than the more definite, two-colour cotton-tablecloth-style checks that could dominate a quilt and prove problematic when you want to bring other fabrics into the mix. Quilting cottons featuring reproductions of historical and archive designs (see the Fall Leaves quilt on page 88) look particularly good with subdued and traditional wool checks, as they tend to have the same slightly faded 'natural dye' look and subtle detail.

Tweed

Beloved of gamekeepers, farmers and brogue-wearing outdoor types, the traditional rough, hairy tweed is famous for being warm and incredibly hardwearing. It is also immensely subtle and beautiful due to the way in which the colours are blended and mixed. Unlike many checked wool fabrics that use solid colours, tweeds often have a mixture of yarns within yarns and very clever shading and colour patterns within the design. If you look carefully, you will often find all kinds of surprises: purples, oranges and emerald greens, and all sorts of natural sea, sky and earth shades.

The best tweeds are heavy and use thick yarns, which means they can fray very quickly and easily. However, they do look amazing in quilts; the trick is to cut them quickly and handle them as little as possible. You may want to use pinking shears or a pinking blade on a rotary cutter when cutting out, or even allow a 1/2in (1cm) seam allowance. (If you do this, cut out all the fabrics with the same allowance.) A quilt made from just nine or twelve large squares of a number of different heavy tweeds would look wonderful, and the little streaks of brilliant colour in the weave would be an invitation to use some bright quilting threads.

Harris tweed

Although there are many regional tweeds (such as Irish, Donegal and Cambrian), Harris tweed is probably the most famous. It is also the only tweed still being made by hand on the Hebridean islands of Harris and Lewis off the coast of Scotland. It is made entirely from Scottish wool and has its own 'Harris tweed' label to denote authenticity. The yarns are dyed with natural dyes made from local dyestuffs, and create wonderfully subtle hues.

Harris tweed is expensive to buy by the metre, but there are sellers on eBay who offer mixed bags of off-cuts that are good starting points for a quilt (see the Wardrobe quilt on page 118). Alternatively, buy a single piece to inspire a quilt, and supplement it with other fabrics, such as velvet, cord and cotton (see the Warp and Weft quilt on page 114). You could also cut up Harris tweed garments found in charity shops and jumble sales.

Harris tweed needs to be handled with care (see general notes on tweed, above). It is worth pinning the edges to be sewn together to avoid any extra movement and pulling that might lead to fraying.

Suiting

Suiting is a marvellous fabric for quilts. It's light, beautifully made, cuts well, is easy to handle and sew, and doesn't create bulky seams. 'Suiting' refers to any woven wool fabric that is intended for clothing. It is usually long-lasting and crease-resistant, with an excellent handle and drape.

It is most often 100 per cent wool (merino wool is the highest quality) and there are some lovely ultra-soft, wool/cashmere blends. It also often has the added bonus of distinctive selvedges that proclaim the fabric's quality and provenance. These can be incorporated into the quilt; just fussy-cut to get the wording into a piece.

Although these fabrics are often expensive, they are much wider than most quilting cottons, and you don't need a lot if you are mixing a suiting fabric with other types of fabric; even a 4in (10cm) strip would provide plenty of small squares. It's worth looking for end-of-roll pieces, as these are often sold off cheaply.

Alternatively, use old wool suits and skirts, cutting out the best bits (it is usually worth washing or dry-cleaning any clothes you plan to recycle before you cut them up). Charity shops are a great source of second-hand clothing and can yield some amazing vintage and not-so-vintage wool fabrics in garments. And, as ever when it comes to fabrics, eBay has plenty of excellent suiting fabric, often sold in small cuts.

Tartan

Tartan fabric is a woven woollen fabric with distinctive and often historical colours and patterns that can be hardwearing and heavyweight (for example, for bagpipes, blankets, kilts and coats) or medium-weight and softer (for trousers, suits or dressing gowns).

Although a kilt tartan could be used in a quilt, it is probably a little too heavy, weatherproof and windproof for the average indoor quilt. On the other hand, a few large squares of richly coloured tartans in what could be a tartan sampler quilt or a tartan family tree quilt could make a really unusual and very long-lasting quilt for outdoors (hunting, shooting and fishing, and all that). Alternatively, use medium-weight tartans that are easier to handle and more suitable for a quilt that will be used indoors (see Scottish Log Cabin, page 100).

When quilting with tartans, it's important to be as accurate as possible with cutting and sewing, as any wonkiness will be immediately apparent due to the linear nature of the design. This can be a little difficult with good-quality smooth wool fabric that has a tendency to distort as you handle it, so do bear this is mind. If, however, you are cutting out lots of small pieces to make a big Scottish tartan statement, the straightness of your lines won't be as crucial.

Velvet

Velvet is both a treat and a bit of a headache to quilt with. Silk velvet is beautiful but very expensive and difficult to handle, so look for medium-weight cotton velvet instead. (Heavy velvet can also be used, but it does create bulky seams.)

Velvet's pile gives it its distinctive and luxurious plushness, its ridiculously soft texture and its wonderful depth of colour. The pile also causes it to move slightly whenever two right sides are facing, which makes it a little hard to keep two edges together when sewing. Velvet also frays easily.

However, if you can take care when using it, and pin before machine-sewing, velvet is an incredibly rewarding fabric (see the Harlequin quilt on page 128). I would recommend using large and/or very simple shapes, and mixing them with other fabrics if the idea of a whole quilt in velvet is too much.

Velveteen

Velveteen has often been seen as a poor man's velvet, but this overlooks the fabric's specific attributes. Good velveteen is made with cotton, and the lighter examples (rather than the tough, often synthetic velveteen furnishing fabrics) look lovely in quilts. Velveteen is easy to use as its structure means it frays less and is more stable than velvet. It is also easy to wash, iron and care for.

These days, it's possible to find some beautiful printed velveteens in a good weight for quilting. In fact, such is its appeal, more designers are coming to appreciate the qualities of velveteen as a base fabric (the shorter pile means it is more suited to printing than velvet) and are creating designs for craft and general sewing.

Corduroy

Any kind of woven cotton corduroy, from thick, jumbo, elephant cord to fine needlecord, is useful for quilting. It's soft, washable, light enough despite its thickness, and adds great texture and visual depth.

It's easy enough to find rolls of cord in fabric shops and department stores, but you may find enough to put into a quilt from cutting up old trousers, skirts and jackets (see the Wardrobe quilt on page 118). A quilt made entirely from corduroy would be interesting, but if you can get hold of only a few pieces, use them here and there in a quilt to add contrast to other fabrics. Corduroy also makes an excellent backing fabric if you want to add extra weight and warmth to a quilt, plus it has great 'sticking' properties so it doesn't slip off beds or settees too easily. The only thing you have to be careful about when quilting with cord is that the fabric can widen and stretch across the wales (the furry ridges) when cut (this doesn't affect the length of the fabric). Either pin before sewing or take extra care when feeding the fabric under the needle.

When it comes to quilting, it's best to make stitches across the wales rather than along their length (it's easy for the quilting stitches to disappear into the furrows, and they don't look quite right on top of the wales). Alternatively, tie the quilt (see page 144); this works especially well with plain cord quilts.

Canvas

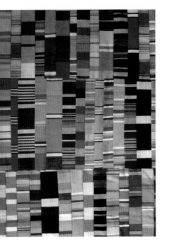

Most canvas produced for practical purposes is too tough and heavy to use in quilts. But there is a huge range of weights, so it is possible to find canvases suitable for quilting. However, I recommend always feeling a canvas before committing to using it, or even making a sample block to test how easy it is to handle and sew. If it is light enough to go through your machine without needing special thread or needles, then it's okay to use. Do bear in mind, though, that canvas has a very tight weave that makes it hardwearing, strong and firm, and means you need to cut and line up pieces accurately.

Deckchair canvas is an example of a canvas that can be used in quilts. It is 100 per cent cotton, with woven (as opposed to printed) stripes in all sorts of colours. It makes a hardwearing and extremely stripy quilt (see the Deckchair Stripes quilt on page 122), but is a little too thick to hand-quilt with ease and comfort, so tying (see page 144) is the best way to hold the three layers together.

Ticking

Ticking is another firm, tightly woven, hardwearing and practical fabric, originally intended for mattresses and pillows. It has a distinctive stripe woven into the cotton, and is usually a single sober colour (such as black, navy, dark red or bottle green) in a regular pattern of thick and/or thin stripes on ecru. Some tickings are simply too thick for quilts, but lighter ones are excellent.

Ticking has become a tasteful choice of furnishing fabric in the last twenty years; there is now a wide range of tickings to choose from and most of them are still very traditional in their stripe patterns and colours. Some have more than two colours, which makes them look less traditional. I still don't think you can beat the very simple, very striking versions with thin black or navy stripes on ecru. Ticking can be a little tough on the hand when quilting, so you may want to consider tying (see page 144) or machine-quilting.

There are also now a few 'ticking'-style fabrics being sold by quilt fabric shops and websites. These are still two-colour, but are much lighter and softer and suitable for general cotton quilts. They might be called – tautologically – 'Striped Ticking' or 'French Ticking Stripes'. Some have woven stripes; others have less authentic printed stripes.

Needlepoint

This is not your average quilting fabric, perhaps, but abandoned or incomplete needlepoint can be used to make a quilt (see the Needlepoint Squares quilt on page 34). It's best to look for finer needlepoint (up to ten holes or stitches per inch), as anything thicker can be unwieldy and create very bulky seams.

Use decent-quality needlepoint that you are happy to show off, and avoid anything that smells unpleasant or is worn out or damaged. Cut out the areas you like or that are useful and feature them either in a needlepoint-only quilt or as focal points in a mixed-fabric quilt.

Remember that cutting and sewing through the dense wool stitching and the tough base canvas will wear out your cutting blade and sewing machine needle, both of which will probably need replacing afterwards.

As soon as you have cut out pieces (which need to be of a reasonable size to avoid lots of bulky seams), it's best to zigzag-stitch all round the outside edges to prevent the stitching from undoing and fraying.

There is no point in quilting needlepoint as it is already full of stitches. Instead, you can tie it (see page 144) with tapestry wools.

Flannel/brushed cotton

Brushed cotton and flannel are the same thing (although there may be some mix-up as flannel is also a term for a wool fabric generally used to make men's trousers). It is worth considering for a quilt, especially now that there are more designs available beyond the predictable children's pyjama bunnies and flowers. However, as there are always plenty of pastel shades around, this fabric is ideal for making a nursery quilt that is soft, warm and washable.

Brushed cotton is a little heavier than quilting cottons, and works well in large pieces or as a backing fabric (the brushed surface ensures it stays put and doesn't slip off). It's easy to handle and cut, requiring no special considerations.

Silks

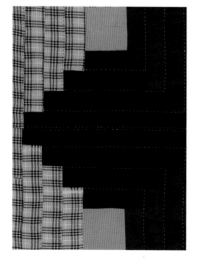

There is no doubt that silk quilts are absolutely beautiful – luxurious, lustrous, gleaming and gorgeous. I've made a couple so far in huge squares in rich jewel-like tones with big, colourful stitches, but in this book I have mixed silk with other fabrics and found that it works beautifully – even in small amounts it adds a lovely richness and lustre.

The widely available dupion and light shantung silks are less expensive than you might think, especially when you take into account the generous widths. Shops often have a minimum 4in (10cm) cut, and if you buy strips in several colours, they will go a long way in a mixed-fabric quilt.

Silk has very little 'give' so needs to be cut accurately. Although it cuts beautifully, it tends to slip, so you need to ensure your edges are all lined up accurately before cutting, and to make sure when sewing that it's not slipping under or away from the needle. It can fray quite quickly, so it's best to handle it as little as possible. Avoid steam when ironing, as water can leave marks on some silks. Silk is not machine-washable, so a quilt containing any amount of silk will need to be dry-cleaned.

Having said all this, silk is not a difficult fabric to quilt with, and I am more than happy to trade a little trickiness in return for gorgeous colours and effects.

APPLES WITH APPLES

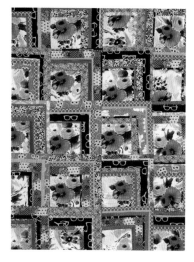

I wasn't looking for it, but when I came across a roll of the most beautiful cotton velveteen that was unlike anything I'd ever seen, with big scarlet flowers and flashes and splashes of lime green and black, it was practically shouting 'Quilt me!' at me. So I bought two metres, marvelled at the soft, smooth texture and bold design, stowed it away in a drawer, took it out time and again to admire it and to stroke its smooth surface – and failed to come up with a good way to use it.

However, a scarlet/cranberry and lime quilt had been on my quilt list for quite some time, and I saw that this fabric was perfect for this project. I'd put together a group of fabrics that kept to a restricted and very striking palette: apple red, apple green, black and white. But even though I had all I needed to make a quilt, for a long time I suffered from a common quilters' problem: the reluctance to cut into a favourite fabric. It's ridiculous really, but a lovely fabric can cause a kind of paralysis, a fear of not doing justice to it. In the end, though, if you want to see it in a quilt, you will have to cut it. But before you do so, it's best to have a clear idea of what you are going to do with it.

The colours in this velveteen make me salivate; I love these bright, fruity shades, which make me think of crisp apples. I decided to cut out the best parts of the fabric that included these juicy colours and use these squares as the focal points in a half log cabin or 'housetop' design.

I discovered that once you know what you are doing, it suddenly becomes possible to contemplate the moment of cutting into a fabric you have been keeping for a long time. It also makes it easier to decide what should go with the 'star' fabric. I combined mine with a number of deep apple reds and vivid Granny Smith limes, a lustrous scarlet silk, prints with black and white in them, and a stand-out graphic print with large white spectacles on a black background; this adds a touch of humour and also acts as a kind of 'scaffolding' that holds up the quilt.

Velveteen is a wonderful fabric to quilt with. It's soft and bouncy but very well behaved and doesn't have any of the problems associated with velvet (such as slipping and fraying). Not surprisingly, more designers and companies are seeing its potential and there are now some really beautiful printed velveteens on the market.

I used an IKEA fabric with a hand-drawn house design for the backing (IKEA stocks many fantastically good value cotton fabrics that are great for both quilt tops and backs). I hadn't planned for my housetop top to have a housetop back, but as I had the fabric already, it seemed sensible to use it even though it had been intended for a different quilt. The binding is made with fresh lime fabric by Jennifer Paganelli. The name 'Apples with Apples' comes from the expression of comparing 'apples with apples' (or like with like), as the quilt combines apple colours with more apple colours.

DESIGN

The design is a half log cabin, which is also known by the Gee's Bend quilters – with whom it has been very popular – as a 'housetop'. This allows the best, apple-fresh parts of the velveteen to be shown off and surrounded by complementary colours and fabrics. The design also enables the quilter to use many different fabrics in strips – from the tiniest scrap upwards.

The fabrics

As well as the velveteen from The Cloth House (see Resources, page 151), I used:
Glasses: Echino Ni-co collection 'Glasses' by Etsuko Furuya for Kokka (90 per cent cotton, 10 per cent linen).
Criss-cross feedsack: 'Punctuation' by American Jane Patterns Sandy Klop for Moda.
Roses in columns: 'Spots and Blooms' by Cosmo Textiles.
Black leaves and red roses: 'Mystic Roses' by Cosmo Textiles.
Red silk: tiny red dots by Moda.
'Aboriginal Dots' in lime by Kaffe Fassett.
Lime and white print: Jennifer Paganelli 'Casey Scroll' Sis Boom Basics from Free Spirit.
White rings on grey: Robert Kaufman Metro Living 'Circles'.
Small amount of a 'Katie Jump Rope' daisy posy fabric by Denyse Schmidt.
'Pop Garden Peonies' by Heather Bailey for Free Spirit.

The blocks

I used 8in (20cm) main squares (finished measurement), as this was a good size with a little bit of fussy-cutting to include plenty of the scarlet, poppy and peony flowers. I could have made full log cabin blocks with strips, like frames, on all four sides, but I felt this would have made the top too static and over-worked. I started by experimenting with strips that were all the same thickness (2in/5cm when sewn), but I could see that it was all rather stolid and unexciting, plus some of the fabrics (for example, the limes) did not work in thick lines. So I changed my plans and used a variation of thicknesses for the strips (from ½in/1cm to 2in/5cm), with the more solid fabrics (lime greens, red silk, red tiny dots) in thin pieces to add lines of colour rather than pattern. Amazingly, the bold black Echino glasses design worked brilliantly in thick strips (and also in thinner strips); this became the 'skeleton' or 'scaffold' fabric, the one that holds everything together visually. The use of the strips varies from block to block, but all blocks have five or six strips in total and make a 6in (15cm) finished width, so each block is 14 x 14in (35.5 x 35.5cm) in the finished quilt.

It is worth making a trial block before cutting out too many fabrics; the problem with log cabin and half log cabin (or housetop) quilts is that they can't be laid out in advance of sewing, because you are using strips rather than set-size pieces all the time. In this version the problem is compounded by the fact that each block is different and made individually. Making them is quite laborious and time-consuming, but also fascinating and interesting as you see just how many permutations are possible.

Once I'd made the component blocks, I laid them out. At this point I could have used a more unusual Gee's Bend-style layout in which a few blocks are moved through a number of rotations so that not all the blocks are set in the same way. I did in fact create one layout this way and it looked good, but I decided to stick with the arrangement shown because in the end it simply looked better. It also meant that the flowers in the main squares were all the right way up; if it had been a more abstract pattern this would not have mattered. The quilt did not need a border as it is already full of interest.

The stitching

The quilt did not need a border, as it's full enough as it is. Instead, I simply hand-quilted with lime and scarlet cotton perlé 8 threads, using the colour of thread that seemed appropriate to the fabric being stitched. I used the seam lines as guides and stitched just inside the squares and most of the strips.

Layout illustration: the quilt has four blocks across and five blocks down, with no border. Each half log cabin block is pieced differently.

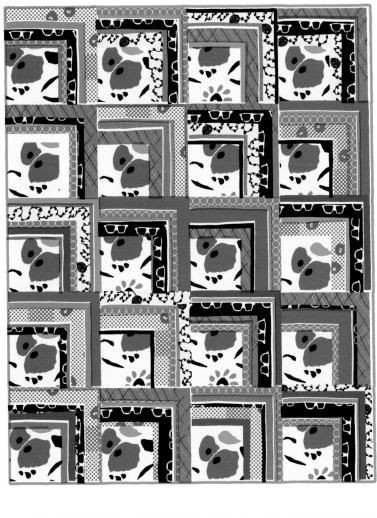

Block illustration: The 'housetop' design allowed me to experiment with using strips in different thicknesses to partly frame the main floral motifs. The strips vary in thickness from ½in (1cm) to 2in (5cm), and I focused on using fabrics that would add lines of colour rather than pattern.

MATERIALS

Fabric suggestions

Velveteen, lightweight cottons, cotton and linen mixes, silk, linen.

This is a fabric-hungry quilt because of all the seam allowances. It also uses a large amount of sewing cotton thread.

Quilt top: if you are using one fabric for the twenty main squares, you will need 1¼yd (1m) of that fabric 42in (110cm) wide. If you plan to fussy-cut part of the design you will need to allow more for this – maybe 1½–1¾yd (1.25–1.5m). You will also need 2½yd (2.25m) of an assortment of fabrics 42in (110cm) wide (see Fabric suggestions, above). For the strips you need 20in (50cm) each of at least four striking 'main' fabrics (with large-scale or eye-catching designs) and smaller amounts of six to eight 'fillers' and 'solids' (fabrics with very small patterns or no pattern at all). Or, if you are making the whole quilt with an assortment of fabrics, you will need a total of 3½yd (3.25m) of fabrics, 42in (110cm) wide (see Fabric suggestions, left).

Backing: you will need 3½yd (3.25m) of fabric, 42in (110cm) wide.

Binding: you will need 15in (38cm) of fabric, 42in (110cm) wide.

You will also need

A piece of wadding 3–4in (8–10cm) larger all round than the quilt top; I used 100 per cent organic cotton with scrim.

100 per cent cotton all-purpose sewing thread for the machine piecing and for attaching the binding. Thread for hand-quilting, such as 100 per cent cotton quilting thread, or cotton perlé 8, or three to six strands of stranded cotton embroidery thread (I used cotton perlé 8 in red and lime green).

A suitable needle for hand-quilting (I used a sashiko needle).

Finished measurements

56 x 70in (142 x 178cm)

House fabric for quilt back.

DIRECTIONS

Note: all seam allowances are ¼in (5mm) unless otherwise stated.

1 Begin by cutting out the main squares. If you are using one fabric for all the squares, it's possible to cut them all out at the same time, fussy-cutting if necessary to get the best part of a design. If you are using more than one fabric, start by cutting out just one or two of each before deciding what is working well. You need a total of twenty squares 8½ x 8½in (21.5 x 21.5cm).

2 Next, cut out a full-width strip or two from each of your contrasting fabrics. These can be anything from 1in (2.5cm) to 2in (5cm) wide. Larger patterns work well in both thick and thin strips, but fabrics with smaller designs or a solid colour are best cut thin. You can cut out more strips as you progress and see what is working well.

3 Working on one block at a time, build up the strips on two sides of the square so that the finished width of the strip section is 6in (15cm), made up of five or six different fabrics (see illustration on page 23 for more details). For example, you could use the following cut-width strips: 2½in (6cm), 1½in (3.75cm), 1in (2.5cm), 2½in (6cm), 1in (2.5cm).

4 Machine-sew a strip to the left-hand side of the square, and trim. Then join the strip to the top of the square, and machine-piece and trim. Press the seam allowances to one side, away from the square. Now machine-piece the second strip in the same way, but in the opposite direction of sewing (so, if the first strip was attached by sewing from the bottom of the side to the top, the second should be attached by sewing top to bottom). Alternating the direction of sewing with each new strip will prevent distortion. Press the seam allowances away from the square after piecing each strip. Make twenty blocks in this way.

5 Lay out the blocks four across and five down so that you are happy with the arrangement. Machine-piece the rows together, one by one. Press the joining seams to one side, alternating the direction with each row. Then machine-piece the rows together to make the quilt top. Iron, pressing the seams to one side.

6 To back the quilt, make a backing that is 3–4in (8–10cm) larger all round than the quilt.

7 Make the quilt sandwich (see page 143 for instructions).

8 Hand-quilt the top with your chosen thread. I used cotton perlé 8 in two colours (red and green) and stitched just inside the squares and most – but not all – of the strips, using the seams as line guides.

9 Trim and bind the quilt (see page 146 for instructions).

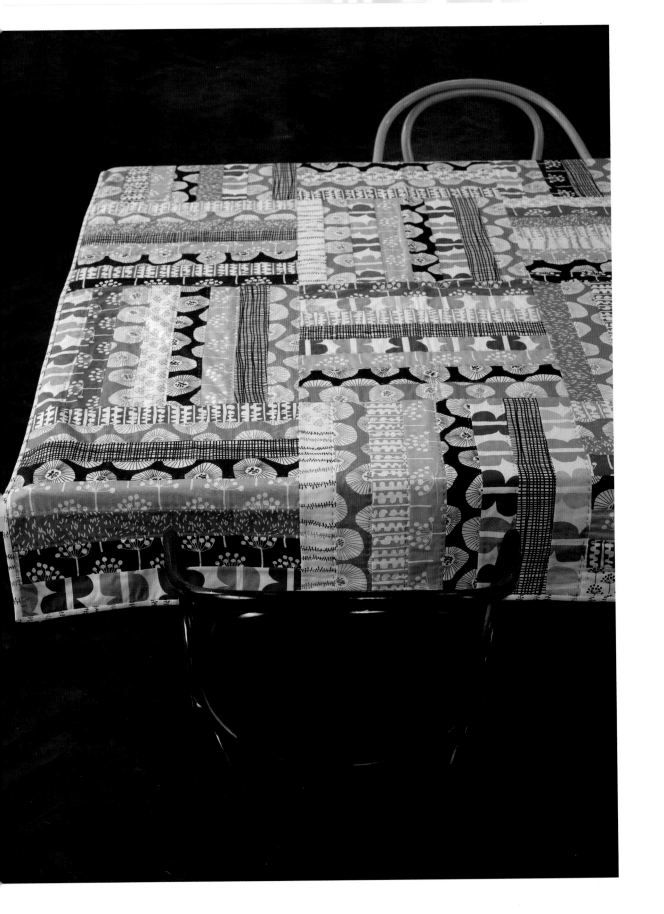

COLLECTION

As we no longer have a well-stocked fabric shop in every town, it is always wonderful to come across somewhere full of shelves holding neatly arranged bolts and rolls of fabric, stacked vertically like books, or in horizontal layers like plates. The very sight of such beautifully merchandised fabric, set out by collection or colour or provenance, fires my imagination. This quilt is inspired by fabric shops and their seductive charms, and by the lovely photos of fabric collections that can be seen on websites and blogs (often the closest many of us get to visiting a good fabric store these days).

A collection of fabrics, created by a single, talented designer, can look amazing and especially tempting when arranged in bolts and rolls, and this can make it difficult to choose what to buy. If you simply cannot make up your mind what to leave out, consider making a Collection quilt so that you have a fine reason to buy a little of everything in a collection. If you need another good reason to do so, remember that collections and designs go out of print very quickly (most manufacturers launch two collections of designs a year and these often replace existing designs – no matter how popular they are). It can be frustrating to discover a collection you love and to buy only a small amount or hesitate about buying any, only to go back later and find that many or all of the designs are already out of stock or discontinued.

Sometimes it's worth buying a piece of everything in a collection – this quilt is the result of me having done that for the first time ever. Normally, I choose a few selected patterns from a collection – the ones that appeal most to my taste – and these I mix and match with other designs. But every now and again, a collection appears that is so beautifully designed, thought-out, coloured and co-ordinated that I find it difficult to resist in its entirety. This is what happened when I came across Lotta Jansdotter's 'Echo' collection from Windham. I could see immediately how the whole range worked together brilliantly because of the clear and individual artistic vision behind it.

Lotta's work marries simplicity, strength and a fresh Scandinavian aesthetic (you can see more on her website, www.jansdotter.com). Her 'Echo' collection is sophisticated but playful, cool but colourful, and is both contemporary and classic in looks. It works because there is variation in scale, pattern, design and colour (there is even variation in the exact shades of certain colours), which prevents the whole look from becoming predictable. It means there is already a pleasing and idiosyncratic element of mismatch and colour clash (very tastefully done) inherent in the collection, which makes additions unnecessary.

DESIGN

After years of looking round fabric shops. plus years of looking at photos of stacks of fabrics on quilting websites, I wanted to make a quilt based on images of fabric in piles and rows that would show off the lovely colours and designs. I decided there would be long strips to represent each fabric, and there would be lots of different fabrics all lined up, vertically and horizontally, just as they are in shops and on virtual shelves. I'd also come across the Lotta Jansdotter 'Echo' fabrics beautifully photographed in stacks, and the piles of bolts – like strips of fabric – suggested an easy quilt design.

The fabrics

There are twenty fabrics in this 'Echo' collection. Five I absolutely loved and bought by the metre. My second-choice fabrics were bought by the half-metre, and I bought quarter-metres of the designs that were lower down my list. I bought the fabrics from a website and when the quarter-metre pieces arrived I found they had been cut as fat quarters; if I were making this quilt again I would ask for all the fabrics to be cut across the whole width as this makes cutting strips much easier. Since making this quilt, I have found that the leftover Lotta Jansdotter fabrics work well with many other quilting cottons.

The squares

I wanted the strips to be as large as possible in order to show the designs, but they also had to fit together to make squares. This resulted in each square being 20 x 20in (50 x 50cm) finished measurements, made up of eight strips 2½ x 20in (6.25 x 50cm) finished measurements. Each strip was cut 3 x 20½in (8 x 51cm), which gave two good-size strips per fabric width. (The blocks could be made up of any size and number of strips, as long as they make a square when pieced.)

I cut just a couple of strips of each fabric to start with and began by playing with them, laying them out in squares, working out which fabrics were the 'stars' and which were the 'bit-part actors'. I'd imagined that all would have equal billing, but it soon became clear that some fabrics were being used more frequently than others. Three designs stood out and – not due to any planning on my part – kept turning up in every block, so that in the end I repeated this grouping. They are the golden yellow, the navy blue and the rusty orange flowers, and they act as a sort of scaffolding or skeleton structure. Also not deliberate until I noticed was the way in which the yellow and the navy ended up next to each other every time.

I included at least one strip of every fabric in the collection apart from a very pale grey-on-white design that was too light to work well (it created a white space that was distracting), so I put just a small piece of this in a strip with another fabric. This was so I could justify the 'collection' idea to myself, but it made me realise that a carefully chosen selection from a wonderful collection would also work well, and that it's not necessary to include every single design.

The backing

The backing is made with four fabrics from the collection and could be a simple quilt top design in its own right. I wanted to show off a favourite design from the collection; I bought extra of the rusty orange flower design as this works well with the top, and the colour is somewhere between the deep and the light designs. I made up the width of the backing with a metre of the bobbly grey design, plus long strips made with leftovers from the top.

The binding and stitching

I quilted with cotton perlé 8 thread in a gunmetal grey and made a row of stitching on each strip close to the seam, so that the quilting follows the horizontal and vertical lines.

The binding is made from one of the half-metre pieces that didn't get used as much as I'd expected in the top. There wasn't quite enough to go all the way round, so I added a strip of a different colourway of the same design to make up the required length.

The back of this quilt could be a simple quilt top in its own right.

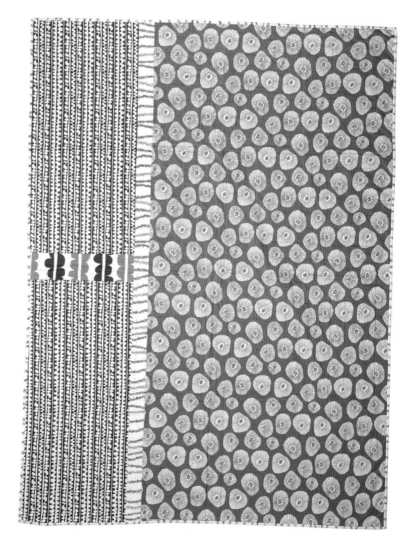

MATERIALS

Fabric suggestions

This quilt works well with any collection of lightweight cotton fabrics. They don't all have to come from the same design collection – they could be from your collection, or a collection of favourite fabrics, or a fantasy collection you'd like to see on the shelf of a fabric shop. The collection could be of any type: shirt stripes, florals, reproduction fabrics… Any group of fabrics that has some kind of link and could be classed as a 'collection' is ideal.

Buy full-width pieces so that you can get good strips out of them. If you are buying a quarter-metre, ask for the piece to be cut across the full width and not as a fat quarter.

You can make this quilt with as many square blocks across and down as you like. The quilt shown has twelve squares (three across, four down), but it could be made larger or smaller according to requirements. For calculation purposes, it helps to know that each square uses a total of 12in (30cm) of 42in (110cm)-wide fabric.

Quilt top: you will need a total of 4¼yd (4m) of fabric 42in (110cm) wide. If you plan to use a strip of a particular fabric in every square, you will need 18in (45.5cm) of that fabric (it's easiest to buy by the half-metre and use any leftovers in the backing or binding).

Backing: if you are making the design shown in which the backing is made up of several sections, you will need the following pieces (also refer to the illustration on page 29): one piece 42 x 86in (110 x 218.5cm) for the main, right-hand side column; a strip 3 x 86in (8 x 218.5cm) to run down the side of the main column; and a column of fabric 20 x 86in (50 x 218.5cm) made from one 20 x 40in (50 x 101cm) piece, one 20 x 41in (50 x 104cm) piece and one strip 20 x 5in (50 x 12cm) to make up the left-hand side column.
If you are making the backing from a single fabric, you will need 4yd (3.8m) of fabric 42in (110cm) wide.
Binding: you will need 17½in (44.5cm) of fabric 42in (110cm) wide.

You will also need

A piece of wadding 3–4in (8–10cm) larger all round than the quilt top; I used 100 per cent organic cotton wadding with scrim.
100 per cent cotton all-purpose sewing thread for the machine piecing and for attaching the binding.
Thread for hand-quilting, such as 100 per cent cotton quilting thread, or cotton perlé 8 (I used cotton perlé 8 in gunmetal grey).
A suitable needle for hand-quilting (I used a sashiko needle).

Finished measurements

60 x 80in (150 x 200cm)

DIRECTIONS

Notes: all seam allowances are ¼in (5mm) unless otherwise stated.
Cut out the fabrics across the width of the quilt so that you get the design
to show as it would on a bolt.

Cut out as you go: don't cut out all the strips at once until you see what is
working well and what is less successful. The quilt top requires a total of 96
strips measuring 3 x 20½in (8 x 51cm); if you cut them out all at once you
may find you don't like the way they are working, so it's best to let the quilt
develop organically.

You will probably not see what is working well until you start laying out the
strips. I recommend laying out the whole quilt before you begin machine-
piecing so that you can spot any problems. Start by cutting out a couple of
strips per fabric (you need a maximum of eight of any one fabric) and playing
around with the layout.

1 Cut out eight strips 3 x 20½in (8 x 51cm) for each square: you will need 96
strips in total. Lay the strips out in sets of eight for each square block. The quilt
is composed of alternating horizontally and vertically striped squares (see
photo on page 32).

2 When you are happy with the layout, machine-piece the strips to make
the square blocks, one block at a time. Begin each row of stitching at the end
where the previous seam finished, so that in effect you are making a U-turn
at the end of each line of stitching. (If you begin the stitching at the same side
every time, the square will become distorted into a parallelogram.) Mark the
end of each seam with a pin if you are likely to forget which direction to sew
the next seam in.

3 Press the seam allowances to one side. Make all the blocks in turn in this way,
and put each one back in its correct place in the layout.

4 Machine-piece the rows of blocks together and press the joining seams to
one side.

5 Now machine-piece the rows together to make the quilt top. Press the seam
allowances to one side and press the top on the right side.

6 To make the backing as shown, refer to the instructions on page 30. See
the photograph on page 29 and the illustration on page 32 for the layout,
trimming and pressing the seams to one side as you go. Note that the backing
can be adapted in many ways to suit the pieces of fabric that you have to hand,
as long as you make a piece that is 3–4in (8–10cm) larger all round than the
quilt top.

To make the backing from a single fabric, you will need 4yd (3.8m) of 42in
(110cm)-wide fabric, from which you need to cut a main piece 86in (218.5cm)
long. Trim off the selvedges. Divide the remaining fabric into two equal lengths
and trim off the selvedges. Join at the two shorter edges to make a long strip
that can then be sewn to the main piece to extend it sufficiently. Trim so that
you have a backing that is 3–4in (8–10cm) larger all round than the quilt top.

7 Make the quilt sandwich (see page 143 for instructions).

8 Hand-quilt the top with your chosen thread. I used gunmetal grey cotton perlé 8 thread, and stitched straight rows along the length of the strips of each square, using the seams for guidance, so that the quilting matches the horizontal or vertical direction of the strips.

9 Trim and bind the quilt (see page 146).

Layout illustration: the quilt back is made up of five sections pieced together.

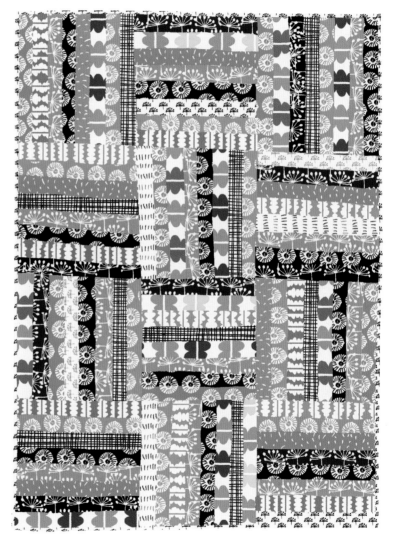

Layout illustration: the quilt top has three squares across and four down, each made of eight strips of fabric.

More great collections and collectable fabrics
These are some favourite designers/makers whose fabrics should be snapped up when seen.

Kaffe Fassett: it goes without saying that Kaffe's fabrics work well together, and he has produced many lovely collections.

Philip Jacobs designs amazing floral collections that would make a fabulous herbaceous border or chintz drawing room collection quilt.

Martha Negley is a brilliant designer whose fabrics are not as easy to find as they should be. She marries great attention to detail with unusual subjects and fantastic colours.

Amy Butler, Anna Maria Horner, Heather Ross and Denyse Schmidt are the grandes dames of American quilting fabric design; any of their collections would look great in a collection quilt. The wonderful Denyse Schmidt 'Flea Market Fancy' collection, which was first launched a few years ago, has been brought back into print as a 'legacy reprint'.

Naomi Ito's artistic Nani Iro fabrics for Kokka (see the Watercolour quilt on page 40) could be combined in a very simple quilt.

Windham produces a huge number of collections of reproduction fabrics (as well as the Lotta Jansdotter fabrics), but it's difficult to find a good number of the designs from any one collection together. If you do, they would make wonderful quilts. The Feedsack collections are particularly beautiful.

NEEDLEPOINT SQUARES

This quilt is the result of my own inability to finish a large piece of needlepoint that I began more than twenty years ago. It was a beautiful Elian McCready panel with huge dark purple pansies; I managed a corner before giving up. Over the years, as I've opened up a drawer and found it and felt guilty, I've thought just how many unfinished needlepoint pieces there must be, and how many completed but unused pieces, as well. So I made this quilt to honour all the needlepoint that languishes unseen in plastic bags and attics, and to give the pieces I found a new lease of life. I also wanted to celebrate some of the amazing subjects that can be stitched, from the artistic to the highly dubious. These designs may not qualify as great works of art, but they make really interesting textiles. The range is enormous, with large quantities of animals (dogs, cats and tigers are very popular), birds (ducks, geese, owls), ponies, Old Masters (Vermeer, Fragonard, Constable), portraits, landscapes, seascapes, flowers, cottages, gardens, crinoline ladies, and too many hunting scenes to count. Although on their own they may not be to everyone's taste, their mix of vibrant colours, clever shading and details means they can be cut up to make something quite different and very interesting.

My incomplete pansy panel was a beautiful and modern design, but because it was on a large scale it would not have cut up well. However, the many needlepoint designs that feature more traditional designs do cut up well. When a section is removed it acquires a lot more interest, and when many sections are brought together, they make up a much more exciting whole. The squares can appear almost abstract when first cut, but together they make a fascinating composite picture, and can look quite different when seen close up or when standing back.

I collected pieces with several general themes and colours in mind: landscapes with water, flowers and flowers in vases, flying ducks, and cottage scenes, all of which look like illustrations from old-fashioned children's books. The colour schemes are also rather old-fashioned – I deliberately kept away from more contemporary vivid brights and sweet pastels.

DESIGN

I gathered my needlepoint over time, each piece picked because the image appealed in some way, so when I came to put the quilt together I wanted to include something of everything. At first I thought of using the pieces whole, but soon found that not only would there have been no cohesion in terms of looks and colours and themes, it would also have been difficult to put together as they were all different sizes. Next, I grouped them into separate themes (flowers, watery themes, English cottages, brown/green landscapes), but didn't have enough of any single theme to make a whole quilt. Plus, I still had the problem of trying to fit the various shapes together.

In the end it proved to be easiest and best to decide on a single shape/size; I chose a 7in (18cm) square finished measurement, as this allowed me to cut a reasonable number of squares from larger needlepoints. Any bigger and I would have wasted an enormous amount of stitched canvas; any smaller and there would have been too many bulky seams close together. I cut out sections and details I liked best and parts that amused me. As soon as I'd cut out a few squares, I edged each one with close zigzag-stitching and they began to look

like pages of children's cloth or illustrated books. I then put them together like a jigsaw with straight-edged pieces. Once they were laid out in rows, the squares regained their clarity and looked as if someone had rearranged the pages of a Ladybird book.

I must sound one note of caution, though. Despite deciding that it was not worth using larger sections, I did regret not keeping a few two-square pieces – pieces measuring 7½ x 14½in (19 x 37cm) – which could have been used horizontally or vertically. It was only after piecing the top and putting back together two squares that had come from the same needlepoint that I realised that the 'double squares' could have been used successfully. It turns out that I cut out a little too quickly and enthusiastically.

The backing

I had thought that the weight and thickness of the stitched top and the richness of the velvet backing would be quite enough and I started by not using wadding. However, the grid of seams showed clearly under the velvet, so I added a layer of wadding to reduce this, and to add a little bounce and plumpness to the finished piece.

I used a wide cotton velvet for the backing because the thick top demanded an equally weighty backing. Cotton velvet 60in (150cm) wide means a single width will work as a backing. Plus, it comes in a range of glorious colours. I chose a rich emerald green (royal or sky blue would also have worked) because nearly every piece in the quilt top has some green and this is the unifying colour that works with the general landscape theme.

The binding

I could not attempt to machine-sew through two layers of velvet and one of needlepoint (it would take a more industrial sewing machine than mine to do so), but saw that it was possible to fold the excess backing up and over the edge of the quilt top to finish it: this is often called 'self-binding'. Once this was pinned in place and the corners folded into mitres, it was easy to hand-stitch the self-binding in place.

With all the stitching on the top, any quilting is redundant. Instead, I tied the quilt (see page 144) so that the knots showed on the back rather than on the front where, in this case, they would not look good. I used tapestry wool, the sort with which the needlepoint is stitched, in a variety of colours picked out from the designs. The clouds of pink, orange and red knots create interest on the back, and hold the quilt together simply and firmly.

MATERIALS

Fabric suggestions

Use lightweight needlepoint; that is, pieces that have been stitched with wool thread on ten or more holes per inch canvas. Anything thicker is too difficult to quilt with.

This quilt can be adapted to suit the quantities of needlepoint you have. There could be more or fewer squares, and you could use strips or rectangles or a mix of shapes. If you only have a few pieces, you could make a mat or a cushion cover. All you have to do then is adjust the quantity of fabric required for the backing and wadding. (Note that wadding is not required for a cushion cover.)

Quilt top: you will need 48 squares of needlepoint $7\frac{1}{2}$ x $7\frac{1}{2}$in (19 x 19cm), each square edged with close zigzag-stitching to prevent fraying.
Backing: you will need $61\frac{1}{2}$in (156.25cm) of cotton velvet $47\frac{1}{2}$in (120.5cm) wide, or the equivalent in the fabric of your choice.

You will also need

A piece of wadding 3–4in (8–10cm) larger all round than the quilt top. 100 per cent cotton all-purpose sewing thread for zigzag-stitching around the edges of the squares to prevent fraying and for the machine piecing.
Strong thread, such as quilting cotton, cotton perlé 16 or double thickness all-purpose cotton thread, to hand-stitch the self-binding to the top of the quilt.
A selection of wool tapestry threads in various colours, or two skeins of one colour, to tie the quilt (this design is not hand-quilted).
A strong, sharp needle (such as a sashiko needle) that can go through the quilt top easily for tying it.

Finished measurements

44 x 58in (112 x 148cm)

DIRECTIONS

Note: all seam allowances are $\frac{1}{4}$in (5mm) unless otherwise stated.

1 Cut out 48 squares $7\frac{1}{2}$ x $7\frac{1}{2}$in (19 x 19cm) and machine-zigzag-stitch around the edges of each square to prevent fraying. Alternatively, decide on your chosen square size and cut out accordingly.

2 Arrange the squares to suit your taste, having six across and eight down.

3 Machine-piece the squares together, row by row, working from left to right, making a few reverse stitches at the beginning and end of each seam to stop the stitching from coming undone.

4 Press with a hot iron and steam on the wrong side; do your best to either open up the seams or press them to one side.

5 Now machine-piece the rows together in the correct order to make the completed top. Again, reverse at the start and finish of each long seam. When you get to the really thick seams, go very slowly and feed the fabric firmly under the needle. Hand-turn the machine if necessary to avoid breaking the needle. Press the top with a hot iron and plenty of steam to get the seams to sit as neatly as possible.

6 Lay out the backing fabric (in this case, velvet) wrong side up. Place the layer of wadding on the backing. Put the quilt top on the backing, making sure that you have the same amount of excess backing fabric and wadding on all four sides, as you will be folding this over several times to make the edging.

7 Pin together to make the quilt sandwich (see page 143 for instructions).

8 Tie the quilt (see page 144 for instructions) with wool tapestry thread so that the knots show on the back of the quilt, not the top. Choose a colour that contrasts well with the backing fabric and that picks out details or blocks of colour in the top. As this is tough fabric to stitch, use a strong, sharp needle, and make each knot separately.

9 Trim the backing so that it is $2\frac{1}{2}$in (6cm) larger all round than the quilt top. Trim the wadding so that it is 1in (2.5cm) larger all round than the quilt top.

10 Working along each edge of the quilt top in turn, fold the backing fabric over the outer edge of the quilt top, then turn under the raw edge. Pin in place as you go. Fold the corners into mitres and pin them.

11 Slip-stitch the self-binding in place using a strong thread (I used emerald-green cotton perlé 16), sewing $\frac{1}{4}$in (5mm) in from the edge of the quilt top.

Layout illustration: the quilt top has six squares across and eight squares down.

HANDLING AND SEWING NEEDLEPOINT

You need to be prepared to:

• Replace the sewing machine needle after making a needlepoint quilt, as the needle will be very blunt.

• Replace the rotary cutter blade after cutting out the needlepoint, as the canvas will blunt it.

• Use large amounts of cotton sewing thread because it pays to zigzag-stitch round the edges to prevent fraying.

Don't use needlepoint that is badly distorted as this will give too many short and uneven rows along the cut edge; these will fray, and there is a good chance that the square will return to being distorted once in the quilt. However, slightly wonky needlepoint works fine as it can be pulled back into a neat square by the machine-piecing.

The squares can be any size you like, but because the seams are extremely bulky, I would suggest that 6in (15cm) finished squares are the smallest useful size. The squares in this quilt are 7in (18cm) finished size.

Press the needlepoint before cutting if necessary. Use plenty of steam – a damp cloth on the back of the piece works well. Allow any damp needlepoint to dry before cutting.

Handle the cut squares as little as possible to avoid fraying.

Sew a firm, close zigzag-stitch round the edge of every piece as soon as possible after cutting to prevent fraying.

A ¼in (5mm) seam allowance works, and although a ½in (1cm) allowance sounds better, it would make for very bulky seams.

When sewing the needlepoint squares together, reverse at the beginning and end of every seam to stop the stitches coming undone.

It can be quite tough to machine-piece needlepoint. It's best to go slowly and feed the fabric firmly under the machine needle. Turn the wheel by hand if necessary when you get to thicker sections.

LOOKING FOR AND BUYING NEEDLEPOINT

It helps to collect with a theme in mind, otherwise you may find yourself with a complete mish-mash of needlepoint. This may work – or it may look just like a mish-mash. For example, keep to a colour palette such as vintage, landscape oil-painting colours (as shown), or pastels, or brights. Or keep to a subject, such as certain animals, landscapes, flowers or Old Master/famous paintings. Even with a theme, I would restrict the palette to avoid it looking chaotic.

This quilt is one way to use up and show off a piece of needlepoint you have partly finished or never framed and are really, truthfully never likely to; the piece could be your starting point.

Don't automatically reject incomplete pieces, as you might be able to use the part that has been done.

It's also best to look for needlepoint pieces that are the same or similar weight. Avoid anything done with thick wool as this will be too bulky. The best needlepoint for making a quilt is worked on 10 holes per inch (hpi) canvas; anything higher (13 or 18 hpi) would be ideal.

Use needlepoint pieces that have been worked in wool thread if possible. Some are stitched with viscose or acrylic thread that looks shiny and smooth and stands out – not always for good reasons – next to wool.

I avoid framed needlepoint pieces that are glued to the backing board as they can be difficult to remove; even if you succeed, there will be glue residue on the back.

I also reject badly marked pieces, or anything that is starting to come undone or already has worn patches, and any needlepoint that smells bad.

The best places to look for needlepoint pieces are vintage, brocante and antique fairs, flea markets, eBay and charity shops.

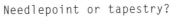

Needlepoint or tapestry?

The terms 'needlepoint' and 'tapestry' appear to be interchangeable, but there is a big difference. Needlepoint is stitched on canvas, whereas tapestry is woven on a loom. Companies often advertise their kits and designs as 'tapestry kits' when they should in fact be called 'needlepoint kits'. To compound the confusion further, the wool thread that is used in needlepoint is sold as 'tapestry wool'. Bear the two terms in mind, and include 'tapestry' in any searches.

WATERCOLOUR

This quilt is made with double gauze, an unusual fabric I had never touched or used before coming across bolts of it in The Eternal Maker (see Resources, page 152), which stocks a huge range of hard-to-find Japanese fabrics. Although I'd read about it, I wasn't really sure what it would be like to sew with; I couldn't imagine how a double layer of soft bandage-style gauze could work in sharply cut quilts. But when I saw the amazing, distinctive Nani Iro designs by Naomi Ito, and felt the softness and bounce of the fabric, I was inspired and used a two-metre length of a floral design in teal and peach as the starting point for a quilt.

As well as the lovely handle of double gauze – which feels as though it has been washed many times and is cosy and comforting – the prints by Naomi Ito have a very distinctive aesthetic, and are quite different from the usual quilting cotton designs. Because of its softness and loose, open weave, the fabric is ideal for the rather blurry, watery designs that she produces (it would never be suitable for a very graphic, clearly delineated design); the abstract and dreamy look makes it an artistic style of fabric.

The analogy with painting isn't coincidental; after realising that what I liked about this fabric was that it looks like a watercolour painting, I found out that Naomi Ito is a watercolourist as well as a fabric designer. Her website (www.itonao.com) is beautiful and whimsical without being fey or twee. Her fabric designs are also spare and confident with unusual repeats that are unafraid of space. It's this careful use of space that makes the quilter hesitate before cutting, and maybe decide, as I did, that it would be best to leave the piece whole, like a watercolour painting.

Should further proof of artistic intent and execution be needed, when you look closely at her fabrics, you see that Naomi Ito, like many contemporary Japanese designers, signs her name on them in a very visible way along the edge. This is not a discreet signature on the selvedge – as there is no separate selvedge and the design continues right up to the edge – but the kind of bold signature you might find on a painting; it tells you that this is an artist's fabric, the textile version of a large watercolour painting. As such, it deserves to be framed.

Although this quilt was inspired by the beautiful Nani Iro double gauze fabrics, it would work equally well with any painterly, large-scale fabric that is difficult to cut up and should instead be 'framed' for posterity.

DESIGN

The painted style of this design alone might make you think twice before cutting into it, but the fabric does not lend itself to traditional small piece or block quilting. Double gauze is not easy to quilt because, no matter how much you try to flatten it, it refuses to co-operate; it retains gentle undulations that could all too easily turn into puckers if you use too heavy a hand or iron. In addition, once it has been cut, edges lose their definition quite easily – the weave has a lot of movement in it because it has two layers that move in different ways. It's a challenge to handle and piece the fabric without ending up with lots of wobbly edges and a great deal of fraying. All this means that if you did cut it into small pieces, it could be very difficult to match up the edges accurately.

Then there is the question of how and where to cut such an artistic design. (This is true of all Naomi Ito's designs, not just this one.) Although with this pattern there is a clear repeat, the flowers are so well positioned that it would be hard to cut them up usefully without ending up with some rather sparsely decorated sections. The more I looked and considered, the more I thought that I should to use the two-metre length as one or two large pieces in a quilt top. I considered splitting it into two widths to go at the top and bottom, with a different fabric or two in the centre (a little like the design for the back), or into two lengths with a contrasting strip between. In the end, I kept the piece as one long scroll, like the Japanese flower paintings that are long and thin. Another reason for doing this was to keep and show the signatures on the edge.

The fabrics
Once I knew that the fabric would be used like a painting in a frame, I could get on with choosing the contrasting fabrics. This is always an enjoyable exercise in scrutinising the fabric and picking out the colours to highlight. It involves bringing out every possible fabric that might work and playing with them, sorting and matching. In the end, I found that it was the pinky-peach colour of the flowers that was best picked out by another Japanese fabric by Kokka. This is a bizarre 'Forest Animals' design with hyper-real photos of bunnies and birds printed on a lovely blush/salmon/rosy-cheek background colour. It is from the Kokka 'Trèfle' collection; it is a 100 per cent cotton, lightweight canvas that has a tight weave and not much 'give' and is therefore the opposite of the double gauze. The strange bunny design also prevents the whole thing from becoming a little too floral and sweet.

I also added a narrow strip of a relatively plain citron/lemony-lime large-spot print from Kokka to break up the top and to add a streak of less sweet colour. (This also matches the lime in the leaves in the main fabric.)

The backing
For the back, I used an organic two-colour shot cotton that has areas of shading and natural textural imperfections that give it a watery, wavy look. The backing is made with two strips placed horizontally and is broken up with a strip of the peachy animal print; this is set slightly higher than centre, like the band on a kimono. It maintains the simplicity of the design and the focus on the great fabrics.

The quilting
The hand-quilting was all done with cotton perlé 8 thread, which makes very clear stitches. I picked out the colours of the smaller flowers in the Nani Iro fabric and used bright lime-green thread on the pink section, and deep lilac thread on the main section. The stitching is done in vertical lines about 3in

(8cm) apart. (If you use masking tape as a line guide, pull it off double gauze very carefully as it can distort the fabric. Use low-tack tape if possible.) I didn't trim the selvedges of the Nani Iro fabric before hand-quilting because I wanted the quilt to show the signatures (and prevent the fabric fraying). However, I did trim the top and bottom edges after quilting, as by this point they had become quite frayed and distorted. With fabrics where this is likely to happen, it's important to begin and end the quilting lines ½in (1cm) or so in from the edge, otherwise, when trimming later with scissors or a rotary cutter, you will cut right across the stitches.

The binding

I added the binding as the 'picture frame'. I used the peach bunny print and the citron spot, placing them so that the peach print went round the peach section, and the bright spot framed the Nani Iro print.

The pieced quilt back.

MATERIALS

Fabric suggestions

Any double gauze fabric that is made for quilting and dressmaking. Alternatively, use a large-scale printed cotton fabric that has an artistic or painterly quality and/or design. (See page 47 for more ideas.)

Although this quilt was made with a two-metre piece of fabric, it could just as easily be made with a two-yard piece if you are buying in imperial measurements. If you buy by the yard, just make sure you reduce the rest of the fabric requirements and measurements accordingly.

This is a very quick and easy quilt to make; it's possible to make it from start to finish in a couple of days. It's also a very easy quilt to calculate. If you work on two metres of 'painting' fabric (here, Nani Iro double gauze), one metre of contrast fabric (here, 'Trèfle' print), and half a metre of a third fabric (here, spot print), you will be fine. Then all you need to do is buy the main backing fabric.

Quilt top: you will need 2¼yd (2m) of main fabric 42in (110cm) wide: I used Fuccra Nani Iro by Naomi Ito for Kokka in teal.
For the contrast strip, 20in (50cm) of fabric 42in (110cm) wide. I used 'Daisy Chain Large Dots' in citron by Prints Charming for Kokka. This amount will be enough for this strip and one part of a two-fabric binding.
For the narrow panel, 1¼yd (1m) of a fabric 42in (110cm) wide: I used a Trèfle 'Forest Animals' design by Kokka printed on a lightweight canvas cotton. Note that this amount also allows for the contrasting strip on the back and a section of binding. If you are going to use different fabrics for the backing and binding, you will need 20in (50cm) of fabric for this section.

Backing: you will need 3¼yd (3m) of fabric 42in (110cm) wide, plus a strip of contrasting fabric 5in (12cm) wide and 60in (150cm) long to make the backing as shown here. Note that if you are using the fabric that appears in the top as the strip on the backing, this amount is already calculated into the quilt top requirements.
Or, if you are using a single fabric 42in (110cm) wide for the backing (so without the contrast strip), you will need 3¾yd (3.5m) of fabric 42in (110cm) wide.

Binding: you will need a total of 17½in (44.5cm) of fabric 42in (110cm) wide. If you decide to use two fabrics and position them to match the seams in the quilt you will need 10in (25cm) of the fabric that frames the main 'painting' fabric and 7½in (19cm) of fabric to frame the contrast fabric(s). Note that if you use the fabric that appears in the strip on the backing and the column on the top, the fabric allowance is already calculated in the quilt top requirements. You will then need 10in (25cm) of a second fabric to go round the 'watercolour' section. If you are using the same fabric that appears in the thin strip in the top, this amount is already calculated into the quilt top requirements.

You will also need

A piece of wadding 3–4in (8–10cm) larger all round than the quilt top (I recommend 100 per cent organic cotton with scrim to hold the double gauze in place).
100 per cent cotton all-purpose sewing thread for the machine-piecing and for attaching the binding. Thread for hand-quilting, such as 100 per cent cotton quilting thread, or cotton perlé 8, or three to six strands of stranded cotton embroidery thread (I used cotton perlé 8 in violet and lime green). A suitable needle for hand-quilting.

Finished measurements

54 x 79in (137 x 200cm)

DIRECTIONS

Notes: all seam allowances are ¼in (5mm) unless otherwise stated.
Do not pre-wash double gauze before quilting and handle it carefully to avoid unnecessary fraying.
When ironing, press very gently and use steam. If you try to make the fabric completely flat, you will only succeed in creating ridges and creases. Smooth the fabric with your hand as you work to keep it as even and flat as possible. Trim the top and bottom edges of the main fabric.
If you are cutting off the selvedge, trim that too. If you have decided to keep any signature or selvedge interest, you do not need to trim the sides.
For more information about double gauze, see page 13.

1 Cut two full widths of the contrast fabric 3in (8cm) wide and join them to make one strip. Trim this to 2¼yd (2m) long.

2 Cut and join the panel fabric to make a column that is 11in (28cm) wide and 2¼yd (2m) long. If the fabric has a vertical design, make sure this appears as you want it to in the column.

3 Join the contrast strip to the main fabric. In the quilt shown, the strip and column sit on the right of the quilt, but you might prefer to put them on the left. Press the seam allowances to one side. Join the column of panel fabric to the contrast strip. Press all the seam allowances to one side.

4 To make the backing as shown, with a contrasting strip set a little above the midway point, cut two 60in (150cm) lengths of full-width fabric. Cut a contrast strip 5in (12cm) wide and 60in (150cm) long. Join these pieces together with the contrast strip running between the two large pieces to make a single piece of fabric. If you want the strip to sit a little above the middle of the back, trim the top section accordingly to make a backing that is 3in (8cm) larger all round than the top, although I find it easier to do this at the next stage when trimming the quilt sandwich. Press the seam allowances open. Alternatively, make another backing design that it is 3–4in (8–10cm) larger all round than the quilt top.

5 Make the quilt sandwich (see page 143 for instructions).

6 Hand-quilt the top as desired. I chose to make large running stitches in vertical lines at intervals of 2½–3in (6–8cm) over the entire top, using two different colours of thread – one for the main fabric and one for the contrast fabric. Use masking tape as a guide for the stitching lines, and remove it VERY carefully when finished to avoid pulling the fabric.

7 Note on quilting: begin and end the stitching ½in (1cm) in from the edges of the fabric if you are planning to trim the edges to straighten them after stitching. Doing this avoids you cutting across the stitches, which would cause them to come undone.

8 Trim and bind the quilt (see page 146 for instructions). If you are making a binding with two fabrics, make two pieces of binding. The first should be made from three 2½in (6cm)-wide strips of fabric to go round the contrast column, and the second from four 2½in (6cm)-wide strips to go round the main section. Start binding with the longer strip at the bottom right-hand edge where the main section begins, and bind to within 4in (10cm) of where you want to change fabrics. Trim the strip and attach the new binding fabric with a ¼in (5mm) seam allowance so that the seam matches the seam between fabrics on the quilt top. Continue binding until you are back where you started. Trim and finish off.

Layout illustration: the quilt top is made from two panels of fabric divided by a thin strip.

More artist-designed fabrics that deserve to be framed

There are several fabric designers who are also artists and who create beautiful, large-scale fabric designs that would work well in a simple quilt like this.

Many of Kaffe Fassett's enormous designs look amazing when left whole.

The artist Howard Hodgkin has designed a small collection of fabrics for Designers Guild. These are simple but on a huge scale, and will probably turn out to be collectors' fabrics in time.

William Morris's intricate and astoundingly well-planned designs are still amazing when seen over a number of repeats. Rowan and Westminster Fibers have several Arts & Crafts and Morris-inspired quilting cottons.

Liberty Prints often commission artists to design for their Tana Lawn collection. These designs would look lovely in a quilt, but they do sell out quickly.

Angie Lewin designs beautiful home-furnishing fabrics that would work well in a very simple quilt (www.angielewin.co.uk).

Marimekko and IKEA both employ artists to design fabrics (see the Big Print quilts, pages 48–55).

Besides Naomi Ito, there are some very interesting Japanese fabric designers whose work appears on fabrics suitable for quilting. Etsuko Furuya for Echino creates bold, bright and often very clever, graphic and witty designs on a15 per cent linen/85 per cent cotton-mix fabric. Some of them are now on 60in (150cm)-wide fabric so it would be possible, and very easy, to make a really eye-catching quilt with a different design on each side from just two lengths of fabric, and in no time at all.

Yoshiko Jinjenzi is a highly regarded quilter who is well known for her ultra-modern, minimal style, which features lots of white space broken up with small details and blocks of colour. For Yuwa she also designs light- and medium-weight cotton and linen blends with scatterings of dashes and lines and blobs on interestingly coloured fabrics; these are very cool, contemporary and understated fabrics. It would be very difficult to cut them up without destroying what the designer has done, as each element relies on being in a certain place in relation to the rest. In many ways, her fabrics are the quilt design, with all the work done for you. She has also written a useful and inspirational book, *Quilting Line + Color* (Interweave, 2011).

The quilting is done in evenly spaced lines of stitches in two colours of cotton perlé thread.

BIG PRINT

Although there are plenty of beautiful large-scale designs on lightweight quilting fabric available, I have often looked wistfully at the even more spectacular fabrics sold for soft furnishings and upholstery, wishing I could use them for quilts. There seems to be a limit to the scale that quilt print designers are prepared to use, so furnishing fabrics may be the only way of getting your hands on extravagantly enormous designs. Although you might not have considered them – some are extremely expensive, and some are so thick and heavy that they would be terribly difficult to quilt with – there are plenty of affordable lighter fabrics that can be used for quilts.

Marimekko is one of the greatest sources of fantastically huge designs. A while ago, I found two metres of a fabric with an autumnal vegetable design that looks amazing in a length, so I didn't want to cut it up. It's a 100 per cent cotton furnishing-weight fabric, but is relatively lightweight and easy to sew. Plus, it's 60in (150cm) wide, which means it can be used whole quite easily in the tradition of 'whole-cloth' quilts that show off the quilting stitches.

I made the Marimekko fabric Big Print quilt first. I then wanted to make a second version with a cheaper fabric to show that it isn't necessary for a quilt made with furnishing fabric to be costly. On previous visits to IKEA I had been struck both by the range of good fabric designs and by the low prices, and it occurred to me that it would be possible to make a single-fabric Big Print quilt top for very little money. I chose a suitably large design that echoed the Marimekko theme and Scandinavian look, and made the second quilt.

DESIGN

I couldn't see how either of the fabrics could be cut up successfully without spoiling the designer's work and the very large repeat, so I decided to use them as whole pieces, as if they were a section of painted canvas. That way I could show off the designs in all their glory and exploit the lines, shapes and patterns with stitching that also worked as quilting. It was a real pleasure to trace the firm, clear lines with thick cotton perlé threads, and to marvel at the clever, stylised designs as I stitched.

MARIMEKKO

Marimekko's designs are so iconic and well-loved that many stay in the collection for years after being launched (a lesson for the quilting fabric trade, perhaps?). Unusually for furnishing fabrics, the individual designers behind Marimekko fabrics are always credited – an indication of the emphasis the company puts on their talent. The design I used is 'Kumina' (in the brown and spice colourway). This was created in 2009 by Erja Hervi, who is known for her playful, naïve patterns. She was inspired by her vegetable garden, and her giant marrows and pumpkins with their huge flowers, leaves and sinuous vines evoke the joys of autumn. The design comes in various colourways, but this uses rich, realistic, deep, warm autumnal colours that can be picked up in the stitching. When made into a quilt, it becomes a fabulous, oversize pumpkin patch that works well as a wall-hanging.

This quilt focuses on the design and stitching, and it would be a shame to lose sight of the stitches on the reverse, so I used a plain fabric that shows up the stitched outlines of the shapes on the back. The backing is made with a couple of metres of a wheat-coloured, organic cotton fabric woven with two colours so that is has some texture and interest, and contrasts nicely with the lines of stitching. I planned to make a single-fabric backing, but it looked too plain, so I broke up the fabric with two very simple prints that are reverse colourways of one another. These pick out the calm grey in the quilt top and have a Marimekko/mid-century/Scandinavian feel. They are from the Robert Kaufman 'Metro Living' collection, which is an endlessly useful source of backing and filling fabrics. I also used the white-on-grey design for a simple, graphic binding.

IKEA

This quilt proves that good-quality fabric featuring a beautiful large design need not cost a fortune. I realised that IKEA furnishing fabrics would be ideal for whole-cloth quilts that show off large-scale and clever designs. I used two metres of 'Patricia', a 2006 design by Linda Svensson for IKEA. Like all their furnishing fabrics, it is advertised as 60in (150cm) wide, although this one has a 57½in (146cm) printed design and a wide selvedge.

I could have bought some of the incredibly cheap lightweight cotton sold by IKEA for the back (see Apples with Apples quilt on page 20, which uses one of these IKEA fabrics on the back). However, I had some black and white fabrics that I wanted to use up, and found that this combination of colours worked well with the black and white in the main design. So I made the backing with two full-width one-metre pieces of very wide gingham (in different size checks), plus a strip of 'Casey Scroll' from the 'Sis Boom Basics' collection by Jennifer Paganelli to break up the checks. As the ginghams were 63in (160cm) wide, the backing was incredibly easy to make.

The binding is made from a black and white stripe from IKEA; such definite stripes make wonderfully striking edges and frames and are worth considering for any large-scale floral quilts.

QUILTING

This type of quilt is ultra-simple to make: there is no piecing involved in the top, and the backing can be made of a single fabric or simple blocks of fabric. Once you have pinned together your quilt layers, you can start enjoying yourself with the stitching, using the printed designs on the main fabric as your guide. Depending on the complexity or simplicity of the design, it's just a matter of stitching the lines you wish to emphasise; it doesn't matter what you pick out as long as you achieve evenly spaced coverage so that your quilt lies flat and doesn't bunch up in places.

It helps enormously if you take your main fabric with you when buying threads so that you can match the colours. I picked out the main colours in the pumpkin patch and chose several shades of cotton perlé 5. This is a thicker thread than I would normally use, but I wanted the stitches to be clear and visible. I found that if you place the stitches slightly to one side of a line, the stitching shows up better as it is on a contrasting background. It's also worth using threads that are a shade lighter or darker than the colour in the fabric, to ensure they can be seen.

Once you have done as much or as little stitching as you like, it's time to bind the quilt. If you want to make it into a wall-hanging, the binding works as a frame, so consider which fabric works best in this context.

The hand-quilted pattern on the front of the Marimekko quilt shows as outlines on the back.

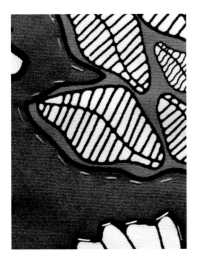

MATERIALS

Fabric suggestions

This is an opportunity to use an extravagantly large-scale furnishing or home decoration design. Choose a big print that you really love and would like to see in a quilt, or use something you have hesitated about cutting into, because you will be able to enjoy it in its entirety in this quilt.

Of course, you can make a quilt with furnishing fabrics of any scale – it doesn't have to be prize-winning giant-marrow scale – and you can just as easily outline smaller designs, picking out certain parts of the design or stitching all of it for a lovely textured surface.

The following requirements are for a quilt made with two metres of fabric. If you use two yards of fabric for the top then when buying by the yard, reduce the fabric requirements accordingly (that is to say, by 3in all round for the rest of the quilt).

Quilt top: you will need 2yd (1.75m) of 100 per cent cotton, light- to medium-weight fabric 60in (150cm) wide.
Backing: you will need enough fabric to make a backing that is 3–4in (8–10cm) larger all round than the quilt top.
If you are using a single fabric you will need 4yd (3.75m) of lightweight cotton fabric 42in (110cm) wide. Or if you are making the backings as shown:
The Marimekko quilt backing uses 3¼yd (3m) of plain fabric 42in (110cm) wide, plus a central strip of contrasting fabric 7 x 60in (18 x 150cm) and a side strip of fabric 14 x 40in (35.5 x 101.5cm).
The IKEA quilt backing uses two 1¼yd (1m) pieces of 60in (150cm) wide fabric, plus a strip of contrasting fabric 6 x 60in (15 x 150cm).

Binding: to make the binding you will need 20in (50cm) of lightweight cotton fabric 42in (110cm) wide, or 12½in (31.75cm) of cotton fabric 60in (150cm) wide.

For either Big Print quilt you will also need

A piece of wadding 3–4in (8–10cm) larger all round than the quilt top: I used 100 per cent organic cotton with scrim.
100 per cent cotton all-purpose sewing thread for machine-piecing the backing and for attaching the binding.
Thread for hand-quilting; I recommend cotton perlé 5 or 8 for this quilt as this shows up well and comes in a good range of colours.
A suitable needle for hand-quilting (I used a sashiko needle).

Finished measurements

Marimekko quilt: 57 x 81 in (140 x 200cm)
IKEA quilt: 58 x 78in (148 x 198cm)

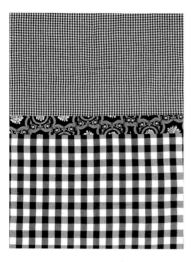

The back of the IKEA quilt.

DIRECTIONS

Notes: all seam allowances are ¼in (5mm) unless otherwise stated.
This is a very simple quilt to put together – it's the quilting that takes the time. It's possible to cut it out, machine-piece the backing and make the quilt sandwich in a day, and then you can start the stitching.

1 Trim the top and bottom edges of the fabric. Trim the selvedges if preferred (I didn't trim before making as I wanted to work right up to the edge of the design). Press the fabric. You now have your quilt top.

2 Marimekko quilt back: If you are following the design shown, please refer to page 53 for fabric measurements and the illustration on page 55 for details of layout. If you are using a single fabric, make a backing that is 3–4in (8–10cm) larger all round than your quilt top.

3 IKEA quilt back: The backing shown is made with two main sections 39½ x 60in (100 x 150cm), plus a central strip 6 x 60in (15 x 150cm), before sewing, machine-pieced together as per the illustration. If you are not using extra-wide fabric or if you are using a single fabric, make a backing that is 3–4in (8–10cm) larger all round than your quilt top.

4 Make the quilt sandwich (see page 143 for instructions).

5 Trim the wadding and the backing so that they are 2in (5cm) larger than the quilt top all round.

6 Hand-quilt the top with cotton perlé 5 or 8 thread, making lines of running stitch and using the fabric top design as your guide. The length of the stitches is a matter of personal preference, so stitch in a way that feels comfortable. Make sure you do not take the stitches right up to the edges of the quilt top as you may accidentally cut them when trimming after quilting.

7 Trim and bind the quilt (see page 146 for instructions).

More big prints

Companies such as Designer's Guild, Sanderson, John Lewis and Celia Birtwell all produce stunning, large designs on cotton fabrics that could be turned into quilts.

Cut-price fabric shops that take oddments and discontinued lines are a good source of furnishing fabrics.

Several quilt fabric designers create wonderful large designs: Kaffe Fassett, Philip Jacobs, Lotta Jansdotter, Martha Negley and Amy Butler all think big.

For further inspiration I recommend *Marimekko* by Marianne Aav (Yale University Press, 2003), the annual IKEA catalogue and the IKEA website.

Layout illustration: the back of the IKEA quilt is composed of three different fabrics.

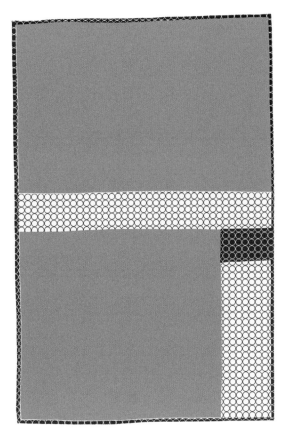

Layout illustration: the back of the Marimekko quilt is pieced from one plain and two patterned fabrics.

TICKING AND TOILE

This quilt began with a box of off-cuts from Sarah, my sister-in-law, who works for Olicana, a furnishing fabrics company in Yorkshire. Like many gifts of fabric, it was a great starting point for a quilt. It provided a welcome challenge for me to see what I could do with what was, essentially, an old-fashioned 'scrap-bag', but a pretty smart one with pretty big 'scraps' that were nearly all full-width and mostly in the form of generous strips.

Sarah had put together off-cuts and strips on a red and natural theme, the latter being a fresh creamy ecru, which is not quite unbleached and not the off-white of vintage linens. Many of the pieces were not technically ticking – which has a specific weave – but looked like it and fitted into that category of practical but beautiful and hardwearing fabric.

The colour combination and the mix of checks and stripes made me think of French flea markets and brocantes, and the popular contemporary, tasteful 'vintage French linen' style in which utilitarian fabrics are given a new, modern-vintage look. They were the kinds of fabrics you might find in linen presses and armoires in gîtes and châteaux, and they also made me think of plump mattresses covered in ticking.

DESIGN

The design I ended up with is a combination of the two reactions I had to the fabrics. First, I wanted to create a quilt with a red-and-white/French/modern-vintage/brocante look. Second, for a long time I had wanted to make a quilt using ticking in strips to suggest a huge stack of mattresses, such as the one in the fairy tale 'The Princess and the Pea'; the strips of woven fabrics seemed ideal for this.

The colours

I sorted out the strips, trimmed them, played with them and started making a wobbly, uneven pile of 'mattresses' with them. I had thought that the Olicana fabrics would work on their own, but I saw that the red and cream mix was looking a touch *too* tasteful. Plus, I didn't have enough for a full quilt top. I thought a new colour might enhance the look, but a couple of strips of a pretty navy and red floral design didn't work, and a more Provençal, warm yellow and red print stood out too much.

So I went back to the original colour scheme, and to my initial thoughts and connections (tasteful, French, Farrow & Ball paints, calm). I added a couple of fabrics I thought were far too predictable – and they worked, precisely because they were part of the same shabby-chic, pretty vintage look. (It turns out I couldn't push the boundaries of the look without spoiling it.) This is why there is a spot and big red rose fabric that breaks up the stripes and checks and adds tiny amounts of a third colour in the shape of emerald-green leaves (this is 'Flower Sugar Red Polka Roses' from Lecien). And because the ticking and this look share a French feel, I thought a toile de Jouy-type fabric might work. I didn't have a furnishing weight but did have a lightweight quilting version. This is 'Wedgewood' [sic] by Whistler Studios, produced by Windham Fabrics, and is a slightly overstated, slightly blurry, impressively coloured and dynamic toile that worked well with the furnishing cottons.

The strips

I decided to use the Olicana strips to make the original idea of mattresses piled up, and cut out extra strips to extend the quilt and add more interest. The strips varied in depth from 2in (5cm) to 5½in (14cm), and were anything from 39in (99cm) to 52in (132cm) wide. (I used full widths where possible, and sometimes extended smaller pieces to make longer strips.) All the quilting cottons were trimmed and left full width (approximately 41–42in/106–110cm). I laid out the strips deliberately unevenly, and extended each side with a plainer fabric so that the 'mattresses' stand out. This plain fabric is cotton summer-suiting fabric with a very fine maroon stripe and an interesting weave.

The quilting

The introduction of tiny amounts of a third colour altered the whole hue of the top. This meant that when it came to quilting, I could pick out the emerald-green in the Lecien fabric (which to me also has echoes of the green pea in the fairy tale) and use emerald cotton perlé 8 thread. I toyed with stitching in red or in a natural or off-white thread, but I felt the quilt needed something a little more vivacious and daring (it would never do to fall completely into a good-taste trap).

The backing and binding

The backing is more 'French salon' than 'Princess and Pea mattresses', but continues the theme of tasteful French textiles. It is made with a large section of the Windham 'Wedgewood' toile, which shows off its wonderful design and repeat, plus a second, more delicate toile, a couple of strips of checks and stripes left over from the top to break up the expanse of toile, and a lovely rich red gingham check cotton. The binding is made with a very small cotton check from Olicana, which frames the whole quilt neatly and smartly.

MATERIALS

Fabric suggestions

Use a mix of stripes with a few dots, checks and florals. I used a simple colour scheme (red and cream with emerald highlights). This could be applied to, say, navy and cream with pink highlights, or black and cream with orange highlights.

Any width or widths of fabric can be used. If you don't have wide furnishing fabric, you can join pieces together to make longer strips.

Choose a plain or very simple fabric to go on either side of the 'mattresses' to create contrast and to show up the strips. I used a lightweight cotton suiting fabric with a very fine, deep red stripe.

Quilt top: you will need a total of 2¾yd (2.5m) of 42in (110cm)-wide striped, toile, checked and floral fabric, plus 1¾yd (1.5m) of 42in (110cm)-wide plain contrast fabric, so a total of 4½yd (4m) cut into strips of varying widths.

Backing: if you are making a backing similar to the one shown (see the illustration on page 61), you will need 42 x 81in (110 x 206cm) of toile fabric, a strip 2½ x 81in (6 x 206cm),

and a column 24 x 81in (61 x 206cm) made of one 24 x 20in (61 x 50cm) piece, one 24 x 3½in (61 x 9cm) piece and one 24 x 58½in (61 x 148.5cm) piece. This is a good way to use up leftover fabrics. If you are using a single fabric, you will need: 4yd (3.75m) of fabric 42in (110cm) wide.

Binding: you will need 17½in (44.5cm) of fabric 42in (110cm) wide, or 12½in (31.75cm) of 60in (150cm)-wide fabric.

You will also need

A piece of wadding 3–4in (8–10cm) larger all round than the quilt top: I used 100 per cent organic cotton with scrim.
100 per cent cotton all-purpose sewing thread for the machine-piecing and for attaching the binding. Thread for hand-quilting; I recommend cotton perlé 8 for this quilt as it shows up well and comes in a good range of colours.
A suitable needle for hand-quilting (I used a sashiko needle).

Finished measurements

62 x 76in (157.5 x 193cm)

More ticking

Ticking need not cost a great deal. It is an old-fashioned, practical fabric that would only ever have been seen in the past on mattresses, and then it was not valued highly. These days, it has become fashionable and therefore more expensive. But if you shop around, you can still find some very good value (and wide) ticking. If you can't find or prefer not to use furnishing-weight fabrics, there are many good similar stripes and 'tickings' (and toiles) printed, or sometimes woven, on general lightweight and quilting cotton.

These are the best sources of fabrics suitable for this quilt (see Resources on pages 151–153 for contact details): Ian Mankin, John Lewis, Tinsmiths, The Cloth House and The Eternal Maker stock all sorts of fabrics that would look great in a 'mattress quilt'.

DIRECTIONS

Notes: all seam allowances are ¼in (5mm) unless otherwise stated.

There are two ways of making the top.

Either cut out/make your strips, laying them out as you go, cutting more of various fabrics as required, then add the two side pieces to each strips, machine-piece the top, and trim the edges so they are straight. This is the method I used – see below.

Or you can decide on a finished width for the strips and make the whole strips first, then lay them out in a pleasing arrangement. This is a little easier, but you may find that there isn't enough variation in widths and positioning (the side pieces need to vary to ensure the 'mattresses' stack unevenly).

1 Begin by cutting out the mattress strips (the patterned fabrics). These should be from 39in (99cm) to 52in (132cm) wide, and 2in (5cm) to 5½in (14cm) deep, all cut in ½in (1cm) increments. (Note that the strips can be as narrow/wide or as deep as you want, and you can use any number of strips, but I would say that you do need some deep strips so that the strips look like mattresses and not just a 'strippy' quilt.)

2 Lay out the strips in your chosen arrangement.

3 Now make the strips wider by machine-sewing a piece of the contrast fabric to each short end. To do this, cut out long strips of the contrast fabric in the same depths as the mattress strips – 2in (5cm) to 5½in (14cm). It is best to cut these a few at a time or you might end up with useless strips. Machine-piece a section of contrast fabric to the ends of each mattress strip so that each whole strip is 63–64in (160–162.5cm) wide. Vary the lengths of these contrast sections so that the 'mattress' sections will stack unevenly. Press the seam allowances to one side. (Don't worry if your strips are not all equal, as you can trim any uneven edges later.)

4 Machine-piece the strips together to make the quilt top. Begin each row of stitching at the end where the previous seam finished, so that in effect you are making a U-turn at the end of each line of stitching. (If you begin the stitching at the same side every time, the column will become distorted.) Mark the end of each seam with a pin if you are likely to forget which direction to sew the next seam in.

5 Press the seam allowances to one side facing downwards so that, when you come to hand-quilt, there will not be an extra thickness of fabric to stitch through when quilting just above each seam. Press the quilt top. Trim the side edges so that they are neat and straight.

6 If you are making a backing similar to the one shown, make a strip 2½ x 82in (6 x 208cm) and machine-sew it to the long edge of the 2½yd (2m) piece of main fabric (here the toile design). Press the seam allowances to one side. Make a column of fabric 24 x 82in (61 x 208cm) with one or more designs: the one shown is made with a top piece 19 x 23in (48.25 x 58.5cm), a strip 3½ x 23in (9 x 58cm), and a third piece 58 x 23in (147.5 x 58.5cm), all unfinished measurements. (Refer to the illustration on page 61 for further guidance.) Machine-piece the three sections and press the seam allowances open. Alternatively, make another backing design that is 3–4in (8–10cm) larger all round than the quilt top.

7 Make the quilt sandwich (see page 143 for instructions).

8 Hand-quilt the top using the thread and colour of your choice. I used emerald green cotton perlé 8 and stitched rows of running stitch a small distance above each seam, using the seam line for guidance.

9 If you wish, embroider a small green 'pea' at the base of the stack of mattresses.

10 Trim and bind the quilt (see page 146 for instructions).

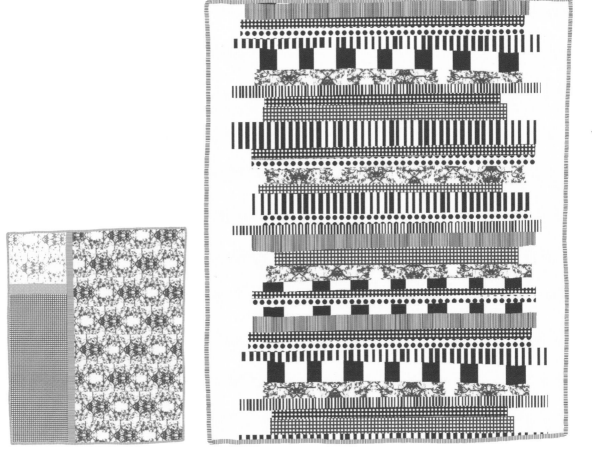

Layout illustration: the back of the quilt is pieced from several panels and strips.

Layout illustration: the quilt top is made from strips of different widths.

VINTAGE FABRIC QUILTS

I have been picking up vintage hand-embroidered tablecloths and textiles for quite a while, and have a small collection of pieces that feature beautifully stitched garden scenes, crinoline ladies, and lots and lots of flowers in pretty patterns, colours and designs. These are mostly stitched on hardwearing, plain white, off-white and ecru cotton, linen or cotton/linen mix.

After years of buying these lovely examples of hand-stitching, stashing them away, and bringing them out for photography and cake-eating moments, I wanted to use some to make a quilt that showed off the wonderful designs, stitching and colours that were worked by previous generations of ordinary women. Although it took quite some time for me to get round to cutting into any of them, in the end it was either cut or consign the cloths to a dark cupboard for a few more generations; the latter was not something I wanted to do.

The embroidery designs on these tablecloths, tea cosies, bags and tray mats either came from iron-on patterns, which were often free gifts with women's magazines in the 1930s and 1940s, or were bought as ready-to-stitch, pre-printed textiles. Some are worked very simply, while others are beautifully stitched with a wide variety of stitches using cotton embroidery threads. They make you wonder at and admire all the skills and patience that were taken for granted a couple of generations ago. Amazingly, these embroideries were often looked down upon by the art and craft establishment at the time, but now they appear quite remarkable and valuable.

It is relatively easy to find examples of these textile treasures in flea markets, charity shops and on eBay, although the prices may be going up as people realise their value. Even damaged pieces are worth buying as they can provide areas of beautifully stitched design. While I have some cloths I would never cut into, I did have some that were torn or worn or stained in places, but still had sections of lovely stitching that could be cut out and put into a quilt so that they could be seen, admired and appreciated.

I made two quilts featuring vintage hand-embroidered fabrics: the Crinoline Lady quilt and the Granny Takes a Trip quilt.

CRINOLINE LADY

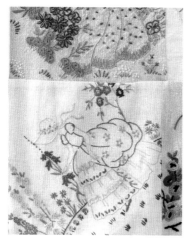

This is a very simple quilt inspired by the crinoline lady, a domestic icon in the 1930s and 1940s who appeared on tableware and textiles in households up and down the country. She was a particularly popular figure on hand-embroidered tablecloths, where she was a symbol of lady-like leisure and repose. I decided to make a quilt full of crinoline ladies after I'd been sorting out my collection of cloths and found that I had more than a garden party of ladies who would look wonderful all together in one quilt.

I have no idea why I am so fond of these ladies, but I do know I like their ridiculously big, hooped skirts that can be so beautifully decorated with stitches, their face-hiding bonnets (faces are so difficult to stitch), and the way they are surrounded with enormous hollyhocks and a wild assortment of flowers that you would never see together in any one garden at any one time.

DESIGN

Once I had selected ladies suitable for a quilt (good-quality stitching, nothing too shabby or loose or tiny), I was faced with the question of how to cut out so many different sizes of ladies and flowers and gardens to make them work in a quilt top. The designs are worked on a variety of scales; some are large and imposing, others are dainty and demure. I considered cutting pieces to enclose each area of stitching, but this would have led to a wide range of sizes of rectangles and squares that would have been difficult to fit together and might simply create a huge jumble of remnants and cut-out pieces.

The squares

The solution came to me eventually, although it wasn't immediately obvious as I was too keen to include all the areas of beautiful stitching. I decided to make the design much simpler and to cut out every lady and scene in the same size of square, regardless of how much stitched fabric I had to cut off in the process. This suddenly made the whole process easy, and gave a design unity to the quilt. I looked at the tablecloths with fresh eyes and, instead of wanting and trying to fit everything in, I saw which parts could be used successfully. It also meant I could include a few quite sparsely stitched areas to give lightness, freshness and a sense of open-air space.

The result is a quilt that celebrates stitching beauty and colour, delicacy and freshness. Once I knew which size square to cut out, I had a template to apply to any piece of stitching. I used my quilter's ruler to see what I got in the 8in (20cm) (finished measurement) square, but it would also be possible to make a little cardboard frame to place on any area of stitching to decide how to cut to include the best section.

I found that the whole thing worked well when the majority of the squares had a similar density of stitching – anything that was too richly embroidered stood out too much. What I included is really the middle ground of this type of vintage stitching: pieces that are well done but are not super-fine and rare; that feature attractive colours but nothing too vibrant and unusual; and with quite simple, small-scale designs that hadn't required too much time and skill of the stitcher, but would still have looked very attractive on a tea table. I ended up with a quilt top that was full of garlands, baskets, small crinoline ladies (some of

whose dresses, hats, feet or extremities I had to cut off to fit), a dog or two, and plenty of flowers.

Trial and error also showed me that it's best to go for pieces stitched on similar background fabrics. If you want a variety of background colours, make sure you have a good selection otherwise the occasional non-standard colour will stand out for all the wrong reasons. This quilt isn't about colour; it's about stitching and sweetness.

I chose finished squares of 8 x 8in (20 x 20cm), so I cut out squares 8½ x 8½in (21.5 x 21.5cm), but the squares could have been smaller or larger. If they were smaller, it might have made the top look too crowded, and taken away the possibility of seeing the motifs clearly (a little framing and space works well in the squares). If they were bigger, there would be too much unstitched space around the motifs or I would have had to look for bigger areas of stitching and larger crinoline ladies, when it's not always easy to find them.

If you are lucky enough to come across a tablecloth in good condition, it's possible to get as many as eight or even twelve nicely stitched squares from it. If you are short of vintage embroidery, a quilt like this would look lovely with a mix of quilting cottons or other household textiles as well as hand-embroidered squares. You could also cut squares out of the good-quality unstitched areas and use them in a repeat pattern with the stitched pieces.

The backing and binding
Both the backing and binding are made from a linen Sevenberry fabric from Japan, which has ecru spots on a golden-tan background – a shade that works surprisingly well with the vintage fabrics.

I didn't hand-quilt because there is already plenty of stitching on the top. Instead I hand-tied the quilt (see page 144) with a double thickness of ivory cotton perlé 5 so that the knots appeared on the back of the quilt. I left long loose strands on the knots because I like the way they looked.

MATERIALS

Fabric suggestions

Vintage hand-embroidered cotton, linen, and cotton/linen tablecloths, mats, tray cloths, tea cosies, laundry bags, nightdress holders. You could choose a theme and collect accordingly – crinoline ladies, or flowers, or gardens, or baskets of flowers, or animals. The embroidered squares can be supplemented with lightweight dress and quilting cottons, or the plain areas of the piece from which the stitching was cut.

This quilt can be made as large or as small as you like depending on how many squares of stitched fabric you can accumulate. The squares could also be larger or smaller. The requirements given below are what are needed to make the quilt shown, but sizes can be adjusted up or down for your quilt top.

Quilt top: you will need to cut 48 squares of fabric, 8½ x 8½in (21.5 x 21.5cm); or as many same size squares as you can cut out of your vintage embroideries; these can then be laid out to create a quilt top. If you don't have enough for a quilt, you could perhaps make something smaller such as a bag or cushion.
Backing: if you are making a quilt the same size as the one shown here, you will need 2¾yd (2.5m) of fabric 42in (110cm) wide. If your quilt is larger or smaller, you will need enough fabric to make a backing that is 3–4in (8–10cm) larger all round than the quilt top.
Binding: if you are making a quilt the same size as the one shown here, you will need 15in (38cm) of fabric 42in (110cm) wide. I used the same fabric for both the backing and the binding; I bought 3¼yd (3m), which was plenty for both.

You will also need

A piece of wadding 3–4in (8–10cm) larger all round than the quilt top: I used 100 per cent organic cotton with scrim.
100 per cent cotton all-purpose sewing thread for the machine-piecing and for attaching the binding. Thread for tying; I recommend cotton perlé 5.
A suitable needle for hand-quilting (I used a sashiko needle).

Finished measurements

48 x 64in (120 x 160cm)

DIRECTIONS

Note: all seam allowances are ¼in (5mm) unless otherwise stated.

1 Cut out 48 squares 8½ x 8½in (21.5 x 21.5cm). It is best to avoid cutting on the bias even if this means that a motif or crinoline lady ends up on an angle (cloths very often have ladies, baskets and posies set diagonally in corners), because that makes the squares difficult to machine-piece without causing distortion. It is better to cut along the grain and have the image at an angle.

2 Lay out the pieces in a pleasing arrangement: I had six squares across and eight squares down.

3 Machine-sew the pieces together, row by row, pressing the seams to one side after you complete each row. Alternate the direction of pressing with each row.

4 Then machine-sew the six rows together to make the top. Press the seam allowances to one side.

5 Make the backing so that it is 3–4in (8–10cm) larger all round than the quilt top. If you are using 42in (110cm)-wide fabric, you will need to extend it with a column down one side. Cut a full-width piece 70-72in (178-183cm) long and cut two full-width 12in (30cm) strips. Trim off all the selvedges. Sew the two strips into one long strip, and machine-sew it to one side of the main piece; trim any excess length off the long strip. Press all seams open.

6 Make the quilt sandwich (see page 143 for instructions).

7 Tie or hand-quilt the top with cotton thread, depending on your preference. I tied my quilt with a double thickness of pale off-white cotton perlé 5, leaving the ends on the back of the quilt so that the thread would not show on the top (see page 144 for instructions on tying.)

8 Trim and bind the quilt (see page 146 for instructions).

Layout illustration: the quilt top has six squares across and eight squares down.

GRANNY TAKES A TRIP

The second quilt featuring vintage hand-embroidered fabrics mixes them with lots of brightly coloured dress and quilting cottons. It's named after the Granny Takes a Trip boutique, which was world-famous in the 1960s. It was on the King's Road, and was initially owned by Nigel Waymouth and Sheila Cohen, who wanted to find a way of selling her large collection of antique clothes. The shop was one of the first to promote 'vintage' and sold Victorian and Edwardian clothes, which, when mixed in the new style with contemporary, tailored garments and designs made from a range of interesting fabrics, created an influential new look. This mix of eras, looks, textures and patterns was a radical departure at the time, and now it's popular all over again. The name, Granny Takes a Trip, reflects the original boutique's groundbreaking mix of vintage and new fabrics; it is perfect for a quilt that contains all these plus pieces of granny's lady-like hand-embroidery – and it makes me laugh.

DESIGN

This quilt began when I made the first two blocks at a quilt workshop with Cassandra Ellis (www.cassandraellis.co.uk). We were asked to bring some inspirational fabric to put into log cabin blocks designed by Cassandra, each of which was made in a slightly different way. I took an embroidered tablecloth, cut out areas of stitching, and made two rectangular log cabin blocks that used a mix of lightweight cotton fabrics to frame the embroidery. I was delighted with them, but didn't have time at that point to make more.

When eventually I got them out again, I realised I could complete a quilt quite quickly if I used just a single block design rather than using variations. I decided on a central rectangle with finished dimensions of 10 x 9in (25 x 23cm), although this central section could have been larger or smaller, have had different proportions, or been a square. I added two strips along each side in the traditional log cabin method. All the strips were cut 2in (5cm) wide to give a 1½in (3.75cm) finished width, but these could be thinner or thicker, they could vary and it would be possible to add more rounds of strips. All in all, this is a very flexible design that can be adapted to suit the fabrics you have.

The fabrics

The centrepieces are cut from a vintage linen tablecloth that I chose for its wonderful vivid colours and lovely traditional flower design. If you have some vintage embroidered fabric, but not enough to make a Crinoline Lady-type quilt, then this design is a way to make what you do have go further by adding quilting cottons (or old shirt or dress cottons). It's a way of framing the little stitched areas, and it's best to choose fabrics that match the feel and look of the embroidery. I picked pretty and fresh cottons that were the kind of thing granny might have used to make her kitchen curtains. Some were new, some were vintage, and some came from my daughters' old summer dresses.

The fabrics I used to make this quilt include:
Red dots: Essential Dots, Moda.
Little violas on spots: 'Sweet Dew', Kei Fabric.
Old dress and vintage fabrics.
Pink and green flowers and leaves on pale background: 'Allure', Exclusively Quilters.
Pink flowers on black/cream background: Antique Treasures pattern 9859.
Grapes and figs: 'Autumn Medley' by Martha Negley.
Wiggly green on white: 'Coral' by Philip Jacobs.
Red and white daisy posies: 'Katie Jump Rope' collection by Denyse Schmidt.
Huge purply roses: 'English Rose' by Philip Jacobs.
Birds and leaves on 'calico': 'Birdsong' by Alexander Henry.
Rings: 'Metro Living' by Robert Kaufman.
Carnation: 'Flower of the Month Club – Carnation, January' by Ro Gregg for Northcott.

The backing, binding and stitching

The backing is made with two fabrics: 'Autumn Medley' by Martha Negley and 'Coral' by Philip Jacobs. The binding is made with 'Daisy Posies' from 'Katie Jump Rope' by Denyse Schmidt.
I hand-quilted with cotton perlé 8 in a range of colours (pinks, reds and golds) along the strips, using the seams as line guides. I didn't quilt in the central rectangles as I wanted the focus to be on the embroidery.

MATERIALS

Fabric suggestions

Vintage hand-embroidered textiles on light- to medium-weight cotton, linen, and cotton/linen mix fabrics are the best for the rectangles. Viscose is an alternative, but it is slippery and can be difficult to handle.

For the 'frames', use light cottons such as quilting cottons and dress fabrics. Reproduction 1930s fabrics would work well in this sort of quilt.

Quilt top: you will need to cut twelve rectangles 10½ x 9½in (26.5 x 24cm) of embroidered fabric to make the centres of the blocks. You will also need a total of 2yd (1.75m) of lightweight cottons 42in (110cm) wide for the log cabin strips, in a number of different colours and prints.
Backing: you will need 2¾yd (2.5m) of fabric 42in (110cm) wide.
Binding: you will need 12½in (31.75cm) of fabric 42in (110cm) wide.

You will also need

A piece of wadding 3–4in (8–10cm) larger all round than the quilt top; I used 100 per cent organic cotton with scrim.
100 per cent cotton all-purpose sewing thread for the machine-piecing and for attaching the binding. Thread for hand-quilting; I recommend cotton perlé 8 for this quilt as this shows up well and comes in a good range of colours. A suitable needle for hand-quilting (I used a sashiko needle).

Finished measurements
47 x 58½in (119 x 149cm)

DIRECTIONS

Note: all seam allowances are ¼in (5mm) unless otherwise stated.

1 Cut 12 rectangles 49½ x 9½in (126 x 24cm), and a few full-width 2in (5cm)-wide strips of several different fabrics. You can cut more as you go along and as you see which fabrics work best.

2 Using the illustration on page 75 as your guide, attach the strips, starting with strip 1 and moving in an anti-clockwise direction around the central rectangle. Trim the ends as you go and use the leftovers in another block. Work in the numerical order shown until you have two rows of strips on each side of the rectangle. Iron frequently as you go, pressing the seams to one side away from the central rectangle. Make twelve blocks in this way.

3 Lay out the blocks in a pleasing arrangement, trying to avoid the same fabrics meeting. My quilt uses three blocks across and four down.

4 Machine-piece the blocks together, row by row, pressing the seams to one side after you complete each row. Alternate the direction of pressing each time. Then machine-sew the rows together to make the top. Press the seam allowances to one side.

5 Make the backing so that it is 3–4in (8–10cm) larger all round than the quilt top. If you are using 42in (110cm)-wide fabric, you will need to extend it with a column down one side. Cut a full-width piece 64in (162.5cm) long and cut two full-width 13in (33cm) strips. Trim off all the selvedges. Sew the two strips into one long strip, and machine-sew it to one side of the main piece; trim any excess length off the long strip. Press all seams open.

6 Make the quilt sandwich (see page 143 for instructions).

7 Hand-quilt the top with colourful cotton threads. I used several shades of cotton perlé 8 in pink and orange, and stitched a short way from the seam just inside each of the strips to create a double-stitched frame around each embroidered 'picture'.

8 Trim and bind the quilt (see page 146 for instructions).

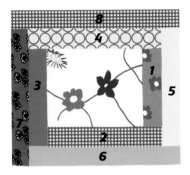

Block illustration: the strips are added to the central rectangle in the numerical order shown.

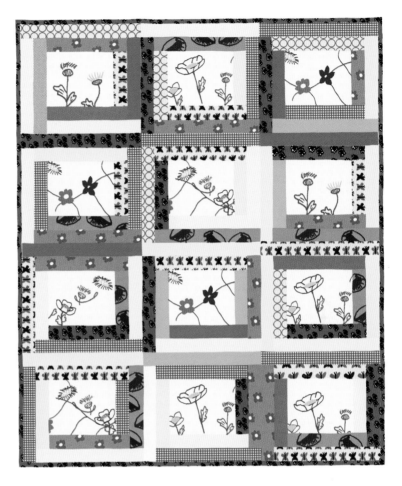

Layout illustration: the quilt top has three log cabin blocks across and four blocks down.

WASHING LINE

This quilt was inspired by a fabric that features a washing line illustration – 'Washing Line' from the Far, Far Away III collection by Heather Ross for Kokka. As soon as I saw it, I loved it, with its amusing washing (long-johns, socks, checked shirts, work trousers) and little birds perched on the lines. I grew up in suburbia where every back garden had a washing line; I have stayed true to my upbringing and use a washing line to dry washing whenever possible. The sight of clothes dancing and flapping in the sun and the wind is a delightful one. This fabric takes me straight to my childhood, my back garden, and the lovely smell of line-dried sheets.

Heather's design has her signature style and wit and gentle colours. There is also plenty of neutral space around the motifs, just as there is plenty of air round a washing line, and I wanted to use a quilt design that kept this fresh, breezy look. I had lengths of the fabric in two colourways; both have an ecru background and contain soft pinks, peaches, yellows, primroses, oranges and browns.

For a long time, I couldn't think how to put the design into a quilt, but I knew I wanted to have pieces that showed full washing lines and I wanted lots more fabrics. I made a problem for myself by constantly bringing together fabrics with the same colours as the Heather Ross designs, and although these are very sweet, if repeated over and over they become a little too sweet and bland.

I'd also made a separate pile for another project with deep orange and turquoise fabrics, including two huge-scale Kaffe Fassett fabrics ('Big Blossoms' and the truly enormous 'Russian Rose') that both feature burnt, hot colours of summer skies and bright flowers. Initially, I thought these would overpower the more delicate shades of my washing line colours, and started by transferring just a couple to the washing line pile. Then another, and another, until I ended up with most of the hot pile mixed in with the cooler pile. The whole mood was overturned and it became a much brighter turquoise and orange quilt with lovely pale highlights, rather than the other way round.

I also added in some non-quilting cottons in the form of deep orange silk and some pieces of a hand-embroidered tablecloth; I wanted to experiment and use all the suitable fabrics I had that fitted in, rather than just seeking out light cottons. So, as with a real washing line, the quilt brought together a wide range of fabric types, colours and designs.

DESIGN

The washing line fabric inspired the strip design, when I realised that the quilt design was in the fabric design itself, and that it should have lots of horizontals with plenty of detail. So once I knew it would be a strippy quilt, I could get excited about selecting the fabrics and putting the quilt together. It also meant I could use the narrow floral borders from a couple of vintage hand-embroidered tablecloths.

As I looked at the motifs, designs, themes and colours, they brought back memories of Stockport in the exceptionally hot summer of 1976, a summer of bright blue skies and orange sun, when for once everything dried on the line. So this is my 'summer in suburbia' quilt, as well as a washing line quilt.

The strips

I went for a 20in (50cm) finished width so that I could get two strips per width of quilting fabric, and I made three columns of strips. The strips are mostly 2½in (6.25cm), 3in (8cm) and 3½in (9cm) deep, with just a handful that are 4in (10cm) deep (all finished measurements). I didn't want it to be too random, and even though this is a very easy and relaxed design, the fabric placement is quite tightly controlled. I cut out strips as I went along then started laying out, spreading out fabrics that were in short supply (such as the hand-embroidered pieces) and taking care with the distribution of the eye-catching fabrics (orange silk and large, deep prints) so that they didn't clump together. I built up each of the three columns at the same time next to each other, taking out any fabrics that didn't work. Once I was happy with the layout, I machine-pieced the columns and made the top. I could have added a border, but didn't feel it was necessary this time.

The fabrics

These are the fabrics I used in the top:
Two colourways of 'Washing Line' from the Far, Far Away III collection by Heather Ross for Kokka.
Burnt orange silk.
Vintage hand-embroidered tablecloth.
Pink on tan spots from the 'Lotus' collection by Amy Butler.
Spots and daisies design: 'Sweet Dew' by Kei Fabric.
Two designs from the 'Katie Jump Rope' collection by Denyse Schmidt.
'Big Blossoms' and 'Russian Rose' by Kaffe Fassett.
'Lilac Rose' by Philip Jacobs.
'Canyon Path' by Alexander Henry.
'Happy Trails' by Benartex.

The backing and binding

On the back, I used pieces of fabric from which I'd cut strips. These are the wonderfully exotic 'Big Blossoms' by Kaffe Fassett and 'Lilac Rose' by Philip Jacobs, mixed with a favourite design, the cowboy 'Happy Trails' fabric, and broken up by a strip each of silk and Amy Butler spots. The binding is made from the two Heather Ross washing line fabrics because I like the look of a line of little socks, trousers and shirts folded round the edge of the quilt.

The quilting

I hand-quilted with cotton perlé 8 in various shades of orange, rust, gold and turquoise, using a contrasting colour on each fabric so it would stand out. I worked across the quilt, stitching just inside the seam of almost every strip, keeping to the seam lines rather than creating a straight line across the width of the three columns.

The back of the quilt uses larger pieces of some of the
fabrics featured in the quilt top.

MATERIALS

Fabric suggestions

Although this was inspired by a washing line fabric, the 'washing line' strip design can be used with any fabrics. Use a total of 10–14 fabrics (my quilt uses a total of 10 fabrics in the top), with a mix of lightweight cottons and any other light fabrics that work well; for example, silk, dress and vintage cottons.

Quilt top: you will need a total of 4½yd (4.25m) of fabric 42in (110cm) wide.
Backing: you will need a total of 4¼yd (4m) of fabric 42in (110cm) wide. If you are making a backing similar to the one shown you will need a 42 x 92½in (110 x 235cm) piece, and a column of fabric 25 x 92½in (63.5 x 235cm) made up of one piece that is 25 x 44in (63.5 x 112cm), one piece 25 x 2in (63.5 x 5cm), one piece 25 x 6½in (63.5 x 16.5cm) and one piece 25 x 40in (63.5 x 101.5cm).
Binding: you will need 20in (50cm) of fabric 42in (110cm) wide.

You will also need

A piece of wadding 3–4in (8–10cm) larger all round than the quilt top; I used 100 per cent organic cotton with scrim.
100 per cent cotton all-purpose sewing thread for the machine-piecing and for attaching the binding. Thread for hand-quilting, such as 100 per cent cotton quilting thread, or cotton perlé 8; I used cotton perlé 8 in several colours.
A suitable needle for hand-quilting (I used a sashiko needle).

Finished measurements

60 x 85in (150 x 216cm)

DIRECTIONS

Note: all seam allowances are ¼in (5mm) unless otherwise stated.

1 Start by cutting out a few strips of each fabric across the width – a full width of 42in (110cm) wide will give a strip that can be cut into two 21in (55cm) pieces. Cut out a mix of depths: 2½in (6cm), 3in (8cm) and 3½in (9cm) deep, and a few 4in (10cm) (all measurements before sewing).

2 Lay out the fabrics to create three columns of strips, taking care not to have the same fabrics too close together and to spread out fabrics that are in short supply. Cut out more strips as you work, using the fabrics that look most effective. Take out any strips that do not work well. Continue until each column is approximately 85in (216cm) long, or as long as you want it to be.

3 Machine-piece the columns, working from top to bottom. Begin each row of stitching at the end where the previous seam finished, so that in effect you are making a U-turn at the end of each line of stitching. (If you begin the stitching at the same side every time, the column will become distorted.) Mark the end of each seam with a pin if you are likely to forget which direction to sew the next seam in. Press all the seams of each column in one direction, alternating the direction on each.

4 Machine-piece the three columns together to make the quilt top, then press it carefully.

5 If you are making a backing similar to the one shown (see the photograph on page 79), from 42in (110cm)-wide fabric cut a main 2½yd (2.25m) piece and two 24in (61cm) pieces. Make up the rectangular section from a strip of fabric 2 x 24in (5 x 61cm) and a strip 6 x 24in (15 x 61cm). Make a column with the two full widths of fabric set vertically and divided by the rectangular section, and sew it to one edge of the main piece. Press the seam allowances to one side. Alternatively, make another backing design that it is 3–4in (8–10cm) larger all round than the quilt top.

6 Make the quilt sandwich (see page 143 for instructions).

7 Hand-quilt the top with a thread of your choice. I used cotton perlé 8 in a number of colours and stitched lines across most but not all of the strips, using the seam lines for guidance.

8 Trim and bind the quilt (see page 146 for instructions).

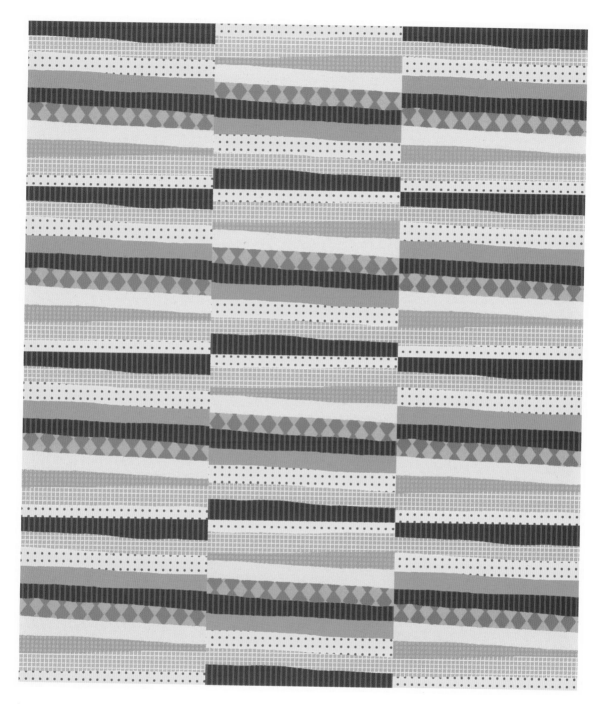

Layout illustration: the quilt top has three columns, each made up of a different number of pieced strips.

WISTERIA

A few years ago, before I'd started making quilts, I found a length of good-as-new, reversible barkcloth in a flea market. It was five yards long, but only one yard wide (it was produced in pre-metric times), and featured a beautiful design of blue wisteria trailing through dark green leaves with warm pink shadows on a clean white background. (For more background information on barkcloth, turn to page 13 of the Fabric Directory.) It was a bargain so I bought it, and even though it inspired me to do something with it, I wasn't quite sure what.

I kept it for eight years or so before using it. The problem with having such a long piece of mint-condition vintage fabric with a beautifully designed repeat is that you think you need to do justice to it, to show it off in large pieces. It wasn't until I put myself under pressure to produce a quilt using the wisteria fabric for this book that I finally straightened out my ideas.

First, I abandoned the three fabrics I'd bought to go with it when I realised I'd chosen them because they matched the barkcloth – and not because I liked them. Then I went through the fabrics I have at home and picked out anything that might possibly work. I ended up with a lot of simple, fresh fabrics: light blues, pinks and an indigo-on-ecru spot. I also included the dusty-pink tea-cups fabric that I knew was a winner the moment I put it next to the wisteria, as it's redolent of the same era as barkcloth: 1950s, Festival of Britain, mid-century modern, and just the right shade of pink to boot. The fabrics in the new pile were all clean and striking, and filled me with enthusiasm, rather than dampening my spirits.

The quilt turned out to be an exercise in matching colours, but also, and more importantly, getting the tones right. It made me look closely not just at specific shades, but also at the feel and spirit of the barkcloth. There are only five fabrics in the top, but they are very carefully chosen. There is the indigo spot fabric (by Mary Engelbreit for Moda Fabrics), a delicate royal-blue-on-white toile ('Never Enough Romance' by Alex Anderson for P&B Textiles), a Hawaiian-style tropical flower and leaf on sky-blue design, and the pink tea-cups pattern ('Vintage Dishes' from the Ruby Star Rising collection by Melody Miller for Kokka) – plus the barkcloth.

DESIGN

Since the barkcloth has such a strong vertical pattern with cascades of deep blue racemes, twisting through the design as wisteria does against a wall, I first thought of using strips. I wanted something that would suggest the flowing, draping growth habit of wisteria, and thought of a brick shape because wisteria so often climbs up the outside of house with bricks as the backdrop. Bricks set in a horizontal pattern wouldn't have worked because they would have cut off the long racemes, so I went for good-size rectangular bricks set vertically.

The bricks

I began by cutting out a few bricks per fabric. These were to be 4 x 9in (10 x 23cm) finished size, which – unbeknown to me at the time – is pretty much the size of a standard British building brick. I laid my bricks out in a simple, standard, offset brick wall pattern (but set vertically), which looked okay but not marvellous. Then my daughter, Phoebe, came into the room and rearranged the brick pieces in to the pattern you see here, a simple staggered design – and she got it completely right.

Once I saw what worked, it was very easy to lay out all the bricks. I created an almost fully repeating pattern except where, on one row, I reversed the positions of the spots and the tropical flowers (I fussy-cut the columns of the flowers so the flowers were on the right-hand side of every rectangle). The finished quilt has eight bricks down and fourteen bricks across. I chose a 9in (23cm)-deep rectangle because you can get two rows of bricks out of half a metre of fabric, and eight or nine bricks per row (depending on the width of the fabric), so a total of 18 bricks per 20in (50cm) of 42in (110cm)-wide fabric. I used 36 bricks of wisteria, so you would need 1¼yd (1m) of fabric 42in (110cm) wide for the main fabric if you follow the design exactly. I then added a narrow border of the spot fabric. The binding is made with the dusty-pink 1950s tea-cups fabric.

The backing

For the backing I used two pieces of fabric I'd thought were possibilities for the top. The first was a beautiful coral pink with an off-white leaf pattern from the 'Wooster & Prince Good Life' Collection for Robert Kaufmann. I had cut out a 9in (23cm) row of rectangles for the top that hadn't worked, so I had to re-piece them so that the section was long enough for the backing – I also put in a couple of leftover spot rectangles. In addition, I had a half-metre of deep sky blue with ecru spots ('Dottie' by Moda) that hadn't worked in the top. To this I added a thin, full-length column of leftover wisteria rectangles, plus a strip of the spotty fabrics, and a couple of leftover pieces of the toile.

The stitching

I hand-quilted rows of stitching across the quilt, just above each horizontal seam, with cotton perlé 8 in a cool ivory shade. If I had wanted more quilting, I would also have stitched along the vertical seams.

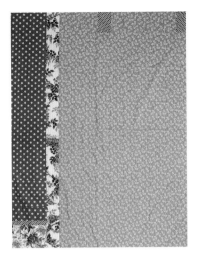

MATERIALS

Fabric suggestions
Vintage barkcloth can be found on eBay, in vintage stores and at vintage and flea markets. If you find some you like, snap it up when you see it as it's not always easy to find good-size pieces in excellent condition. Alternatively, use large-scale floral and tropical prints on light or medium-weight cotton. These don't have to be quilting cottons, and you may find some big designs in independent fabric shops (see Resources on pages 151–153). However, if you are planning to use quilting cottons, you will find there is plenty of choice. Alexander Henry fabrics are particularly good for lush, tropical designs.

Quilt top: you will need to cut 112 rectangles (bricks) 4½ x 9½in (11 x 24cm), which will require a total of 3¼yd (3m) of fabric 42in (110cm) wide, including 1¼yd (1m) of 'lead fabric'. You will also need 17½in (44.5cm) of fabric 42in (110cm) wide for the border.
Backing: if you are making the quilt backing as shown (see illustration on page 87), you will need a 78in (198cm)-long piece of fabric, 42in (110cm) wide for the main piece. You will also need to make a column 16 x 78in (40.5 x 198cm) with one or more fabrics: the column as shown is made of three sections: top 16 x 65¼in (40.5 x 165.5cm), middle 16 x 2½in (40.5 x 6cm) and bottom piece 16 x 11¼in (40.5 x 28.5cm). You will also need a narrow strip 4½ x 78in (11.5 x 198cm). To make a backing from a single fabric you will need a total of 3¾yd (3.5m) of fabric 42in (110cm) wide.
Binding: you will need 17½in (44.5cm) of fabric 42in (110cm) wide.

You will also need
A piece of wadding 3–4in (8–10cm) larger all round than the quilt top; I used 100 per cent organic cotton with scrim.
100 per cent cotton all-purpose sewing thread for the machine-piecing and for attaching the binding. Thread for hand-quilting, such as 100 per cent cotton quilting thread, or cotton perlé 8 (I used cotton perlé 8 in ivory).
A suitable needle for hand-quilting (I used a sashiko needle).

Finished measurements
59½ x 79½in (151 x 202cm)

DIRECTIONS

Notes: all seam allowances are $\frac{1}{4}$in (5mm) unless otherwise stated.
This quilt can easily be made larger or smaller by increasing or reducing
the number of bricks, but you will need to adjust the wadding and fabric
requirements accordingly.

1 You will need a total of 112 rectangles $4\frac{1}{2}$ x $9\frac{1}{2}$in (11 x 24cm). If you wish
to follow the design shown exactly, please refer to the illustration on page 87 to
see how many rectangles of each colour you need (maximum 36, minimum
17). However, I do not recommend cutting out all the pieces before laying out
and machine-piecing. Instead, choose a number of possible fabrics, cut out a
few bricks from each, and begin by laying these out and seeing which work and
which do not before cutting out more as you go along. If necessary, fussy-cut
rectangles to get the best parts of a design.

2 Once you are happy with the layout, machine-piece the rectangles together
horizontally, row by row, pressing the seams to one side and alternating the
direction with each row to avoid bulky corners.

3 Machine-piece the horizontal rows together to make the quilt top. Iron the
top, pressing the seams to one side.

4 Make the border by cutting out seven strips $2\frac{1}{2}$ x 42in (6 x 110cm) across
the width of the fabric. Trim and join them to make one long strip. Machine-sew
a length to each short side of the quilt top, then to each long side, cutting the
strip and reattaching it to the next side as you work your way round. Press the
seam allowances to one side, facing away from the bricks.

5 If you are making the quilt backing as shown here, machine-piece the
78 x 42in (198 x 110cm) main piece, the 16 x 78in (40.5 x 198cm) column,
and the $4\frac{1}{2}$ x 78in (11.5 x 198cm) strip as shown in the illustration on page 87.
Alternatively, make another backing design that is 3–4in (8–10cm) larger all
round than the quilt top.

6 Make the quilt sandwich (see page 143 for instructions).

7 Hand-quilt the top with the thread of your choice. I stitched horizontal rows
of running stitch with ivory cotton perlé 8 just above the seams.

8 Trim and bind the quilt (see page 146 for instructions).

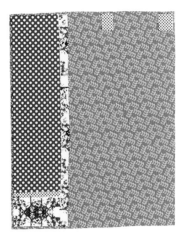

Layout illustration: the quilt back includes pieces cut for the top that didn't work there, but work well here.

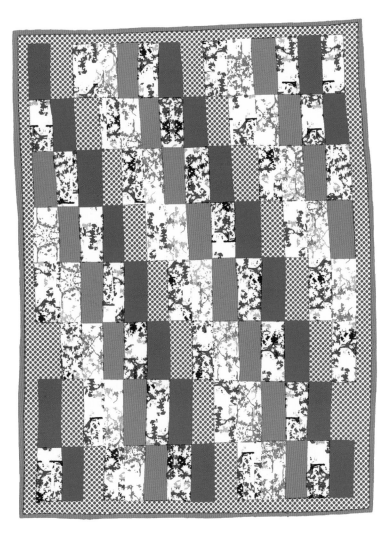

Layout illustration: the quilt top is made up of eight horizontal rows, each with fourteen bricks in it.

FALL LEAVES

The woven wool section of a fabric shop is a wonderful place to seek quilting inspiration as there are so many amazing fabrics created for suits and skirts, jackets and trousers. Some are very expensive, and some are not suitable for quilting, but that still leaves a great choice of checks and plaids, tweeds and stripes, some of which I have used elsewhere in this book (see Warp and Weft, page 114, and Wardrobe, page 118).

This quilt began in the basement of The Cloth Shop in London's Soho, which stocks a marvellous assortment of wool dressmaking and suiting fabrics. It was there that I found a roll of the softest wool check 64in (162.5cm) wide in equally soft colours. I had no idea what I would do with it, only that I wanted to put it into a quilt. It contains the natural colours of an autumn landscape: slightly faded, washed-out shades of blue and russet and soft pink that have been softened by the summer sun. It immediately made me think of getting out cosy blankets and quilts in autumn when the nippy evenings start and the days get shorter.

When looking for fabrics to go with it, I found that reproduction fabrics were the best. This rather muted, history-book look may not be my usual one, but in fact I very much like American quilting fabrics with designs reproduced from earlier times, particularly those from the nineteenth century, and especially the Civil War period. They have fantastically detailed, often very small, designs and a very particular colouring. I made a pile of all the possible inclusions but many had to be culled as they looked too wishy-washy and bland next to the check. I felt that although a certain tone and intensity needed to be maintained, each fabric cross on the quilt top had to stand out and be seen, and for that I needed at least some contrast between the fabrics.

I made a selection of reproduction prints and a couple of more recent Free Spirit designs, and added to them some quilting-weight Dutch cotton chintz. The chintz is glazed and beautifully shiny, although a little difficult to work with as the glaze wears off when ironed and the fabric relaxes and becomes rather wavy.

The backing is made with leftovers. I used a large two-colour Amy Butler 'Temple Flowers' print in a lovely pale robin's egg-blue and deep plum, plus a print from Windham Fabrics, 'Vanity Fair c.1892' by Nancy Gere, in soft and muted colours. The binding is a second Nancy Gere reproduction fabric from the same collection, which picks out the soft blues, pinks and lilacs in the top.

Once the quilt was finished it looked and felt very autumnal. It has a misty, mellow, fruitful character (shades of 'Ode to Autumn' by Keats), and by coincidence or maybe by design, there are leaves scattered all over the top. So it's a Fall Leaves quilt.

DESIGN

The wool check fabric was easy to handle; it has plenty of surface texture and is lightly felted so it holds together well when cut. Nevertheless, like most soft wools, it would lose shape easily if handled too much, especially in small or angled pieces. So it is best to use shapes with shortish edges and firm corners; rectangles and squares are the best options.

The fabrics and the design
This quilt includes:
The 'Old Sturbridge Village Collection' and 'Rocky Mountain Quilt Museum Collection' by Judie Rothermel for Marcus Fabrics; a couple of Free Spirit prints; 'Jo's Calicoes' by Jo Morton for Andover Fabrics; 'Echoes of the Past: Austen Manor' by Harriet Hargrave for P&B Textiles; 'Victoria's Crown Princess Feathers 1830-1865' by Brackman & Thompson for Moda; a Coccinelle print by Yuwa; and several chintz designs from Den Haan & Wagenmakers in Holland.
My fabrics could have gone into a simple quilt of random squares, with the fabrics scattered over the top in no particular order. But because I wanted some definition, I chose a simple repeat pattern in which five squares make crosses. This way, the eye can focus, and pick out the different fabrics: for this to happen, it is worth considering how each fabric works next to its neighbours when laying out the quilt, and making sure there is some level of contrast.

The crosses
I cut out a number of 4in (10cm) squares, which would give 3½in (9cm) finished squares. If I made a second version, I would have 4in (10cm) finished squares and therefore cut out 4½in (11cm) squares. However, cutting out 4in (10cm) squares works well in terms of fabric usage as it's possible to get ten squares across the width of 42in (110cm)-wide quilting cotton, which gives you two full crosses.

The crosses can be arranged in a random pattern, or they can be in a repeat pattern. I decided on the latter as I wanted the wool check crosses to stand out and be the focal point. Because of the way the crosses stack vertically, the repeats end up on a diagonal horizontally, which adds interest. The rest of the crosses appear to be random, but are actually carefully placed to spread them out and to make the most of available fabrics.

This is a surprisingly fabric-hungry quilt, but also good for using up small amounts of fabric. As long as you can get from one to five 4in (10cm) squares out of the piece, a fabric can be used either as a full cross or around the edges, where fewer squares are needed to complete the pattern.

The border and the stitching
I chose a generously wide border to extend the quilt, but also to complement the blocks. Using the wool check was the best way to do this, but I also added a thin border of reproduction cotton fabric.

I hand-quilted with cotton perlé 8 thread in a shade of pale gold. I stitched a criss-cross grid of diagonal rows, using masking tape as line guides. The tape was then removed carefully to avoid pulling up any surface fibres.

MATERIALS

Fabric suggestions

Soft wool checks and reproduction cotton quilting fabrics, or any mix of any of the fabrics used in this book; for example, squares of cord or velvet or tweed would work well in an autumnal quilt. I started with the main wool fabric then added any fabrics I thought would work. I did not calculate beforehand how much I would need, and simply stopped when I ran out of suitable fabric. I find this relaxed approach is by far the best way to make quilts you like with the fabrics you like. However, I give specific fabric requirements below.

Quilt top: you will need a total of 2½yd (2.25m) of assorted fabrics 42in (110cm) wide for the squares, plus 7½in (19cm) of fabric 42in (110cm) wide for the inner border and 33in (83.75cm) of fabric 42in (110cm) wide for the outer, wider border.
If you want to use a 60in (150cm)- or 64in (162cm)-wide wool check fabric for the main crosses and the outer border, you will need to buy 1¼yd (1m).
Backing: you will need a total of 3¼yd (3m) of fabric. If you are following the design shown, note that I used a 2m piece of Amy Butler design and a 1m piece of Nancy Gere fabric cut into two half-metre pieces (and equivalent in yards is enough, so you could buy 2yd and 1yd.)
Binding: you will need 15in (38cm) of fabric 42in (110cm) wide.

You will also need

A piece of wadding 3–4in (8–10cm) larger all round than the quilt top; I used 100 per cent organic cotton with scrim.
100 per cent cotton all-purpose sewing thread for the machine-piecing and for attaching the binding. Thread for hand-quilting; I recommend cotton perlé 8 for this quilt as this shows up well and comes in a good range of colours. A suitable needle for hand-quilting (I used a sashiko needle).

Finished measurements

56 x 69in (142 x 175.25cm)

DIRECTIONS

Notes: all seam allowances are ¼in (5mm) unless otherwise stated.

You will need multiples of five squares to make the crosses, but if you have only a small piece of fabric that you'd like to include, it can be used around the edge where there is space for just a single square, or up to four squares. I recommend cutting out up to five squares of each potential fabric first, seeing what works well, and then cutting out more as you go along. Even with the planned main fabric (here, the wool check), I would cut out just a couple of sets of squares to begin with.

1 You will need a total of 221 4in (10cm) squares, including a total of 33 sets of five to make the crosses. The rest of the squares are required in sets of four, three, two and one (see the illustration on page 93 for further details of the layout).

2 Once you are happy with the arrangement of crosses and squares, machine-piece the horizontal rows together one by one. Iron them, pressing the seams to one side and alternating that side from row to row.

3 Now machine-piece the horizontal rows together one by one to create the quilt top. Iron, pressing the seams to one side.

4 Add the inner border. Cut out six 1½in (4cm)-wide strips across the full width of the fabric. Trim and join them to make one long strip. Machine-sew a length to each short side of the quilt top, then to each long side, cutting the strip and reattaching it to the next side as you work your way round. Press the seam allowances to one side, facing away from the quilt top.

5 Make and attach the second border. Cut out six 5½in (14cm) strips of 42in (110cm)-wide fabric or four 5½in (14cm) strips of 60in (150cm)- or 64in (162cm)-wide fabric. Join and attach these in the same way as for the inner border. The quilt top is now finished.

6 To make the backing as shown, you need a 2yd (1.75m) piece of fabric 42in (110cm) wide, trimmed. You also need a 1¼yd (1m) piece of fabric cut into two widthways – 18 x 42in (50 x 110cm). Trim and machine-piece these, joining them at selvedge edges to create a long column 18in (45.5cm) wide and 72in (180cm) long. Press the seam allowances open. Attach the column to the main piece (to the right or the left, as you please) to extend the backing. Iron, pressing the seam open. Alternatively, make another backing design that is 3–4in (8–10cm) larger all round than the quilt top.

7 Make the quilt sandwich (see page 143 for instructions).

8 Hand-quilt the top with the thread of your choice. I used cotton perlé 8 and stitched diagonal rows in a criss-cross pattern, using masking tape as line guides.

9 Trim and bind the quilt (see page 146 for instructions).

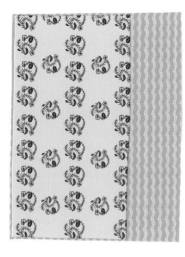

Layout illustration: the back of the quilt is made from just two fabrics.

Layout illustration: the quilt top is made from small squares pieced to form crosses.

More reproduction fabrics

Windham is my favourite producer of reproduction fabrics. They have the most enormous catalogue, but their lovely fabrics can be difficult to find outside the US. I especially like the Nancy Gere designs.

The Judie Rothermel fabrics for Marcus Brothers Fabrics are also excellent.

The Japanese company, Lecien, produces many old-fashioned designs in soft, muted palettes that would work well in this sort of quilt.

Quilting-weight glazed chintz is available from Den Haan & Wagenmakers in Holland. They have a shop in Amsterdam and a website (www.dutchquilts.net).

KITCHEN SINK

If you take an interest in or make quilts, sooner or later you will become aware of the immense importance in textile history of red and white quilts. There is no other quilting colour combination that has been and is still so widely used, is ultra-traditional, yet can be endlessly reinvented, reinterpreted and modernised. Whether it's used in a simple or a complex design, it is always fresh, clean, classic and striking.

I am a great fan of red and white quilts; even though I haven't got round to making many because I've been so busy enjoying quilting with lots of colours, the possibility has always been at the back of my mind. Recently, though, I was inspired to make a red and white quilt by a single fabric with a kitchen theme: the red fabric with beaters, the sort you find on electric mixers, which you can see in this quilt. (This is the 'Metro Market Monaluna' design by Robert Kaufman.) I like it because I do lots of baking, and it seems highly appropriate, but also because it's very graphic and very clever. Despite my enthusiasm for the fabric, however, it's such a specific shade of red that I wasn't sure how it would work with other reds, and so it stayed uncut.

Then I happened to be given a pile of beautiful vintage French linens. They were all plain, unbleached, white or off-white, hardwearing, practical household fabrics (sheets, drying cloths) in a variety of natural fibres, including a beautiful, large piece of métis (a linen and cotton mix; see page 14 for more information) with the tiny initials 'A' and 'P' (my daughters' first name initials) hand-stitched in cross stitch in the centre. They were the perfect match for my mixers red fabric and, as they made me think of kitchens, sinks and washing-up, I realised they could be the whites to go in a domestic-themed red and white quilt.

So I selected the initialled métis and a piece of French flax fabric, the sort you would use on a roller towel, which is thick with an open weave and very soft and homely. I sorted out a pile of red fabrics with domestic motifs – cups, fruit, flowers – to go with them. As I wanted to keep to a strictly two-colour red and white theme to create a bold contrast in my quilt, most of the red fabrics have only two colours, too. Initially, I wanted to restrict the red to graphic, regular designs (tea cups and beaters) but when I did this, the top began to look quite cold and severe. The addition of red fabrics with vines and flowers and movement livened things up and prevented it from being too static. Although the beaters fabric is a very pure and cool red I thought would be difficult to work with, I found that having a number of different shades of red works well and makes the quilt more interesting to 'read', and that the variations give the quilt some visual energy.

DESIGN

There are so many design possibilities with red and white quilts that deciding on just one can be quite daunting. However, I did know that I wanted to include reasonably large pieces to show off the lovely designs in the red fabrics, and that I liked rectangles for red and white quilts. I'd seen some great simplified 'windmill' quilts that used rectangles (rather than the more complicated angled pieces that are more like true windmill sails), so decided to use this design to make a sort of 'red cross' quilt. It's a simple yet effective design, very easy to put together, and if you use high-contrast fabrics such as red and white it can be very striking.

The blocks

The rectangles have to be twice as long as they are wide for the blocks to be squares. Each block is made up of four squares, each of which is made up of two rectangles. My squares are 6 x 6in (15 x 15cm) finished size, so each rectangle is 6½ x 3½in (16.5 x 9cm) when cut. If I'd wanted smaller squares I could have made the finished rectangles 4 x 2in (10 x 5cm), so the cut rectangles would be 4½ x 2½in (11 x 6cm).

Although it's possible to cut out every rectangle individually (and you may need to do this when you are using scraps), it's easier to cut 3½in (9cm)-wide strips of fabric across the width or along the length of your fabric, depending on the pattern (the latter is what I had to do with the beaters as the motif ran vertically). A white strip of the same length and width is then machine-sewn to a red strip, the seam is pressed (press to the darker side so the darker fabric doesn't show through on the right side), and the result cut into 6½in (16.5cm) pieces to create 6½ x 6½in (16.5 x 16.5cm) squares.

The quilt top is made up of five blocks across and five blocks down. I made a total of twenty-five squares using a number of different red fabrics, then arranged them so that they were evenly distributed. This is a good quilt for using up small amounts of red fabric – you only need to be able to cut out four rectangles from a scrap or leftover piece.

The fabrics

The white rectangles are all cut from the one piece of métis plus the linen towel, although the quilt would work equally well with a variety of white/off-white/unbleached vintage linens, or any modern quilting linens and linen mixes such as the excellent 'Essex' fabrics from Robert Kaufman (www.robertkaufman.com).
The red fabrics used in the quilt are:
A Yuwa tea cups design.
'Farmhouse West 1890–1940' by L.B. Krueger for Windham.
'Feedsack VI ca. 1930' for Windham.
'Wee Play' by American Jane Patterns by Sandy Klop for Moda.
'More Romance' by Alex Anderson for P&B Textiles.
'Metro Market Monaluna' by Robert Kaufman.

The backing, binding and stitching

I added a plain métis border to frame the blocks, and the backing maintains the feeling of simplicity as it is made from a single, wide sheet of métis. The binding uses the beaters fabric, which folds over nicely around the edges. I hand-quilted with a rich red cotton perlé 8 thread. The straight lines of stitching show up clearly in a rectangular grid pattern on the back. Red and white quilts have such a classic look that having your colour options limited is a positive; it also makes a very enjoyable change from more extravagant and colourful quilts.

Métis

This is an incredibly durable French fabric that was used for sheets and tablecloths, and came in huge pieces that could be cut down and hemmed as necessary. It was made in a variety of weights; some are relatively light but some are tough and strong like canvas and not suitable for quilts. Today métis sheets are available through dealers and brocantes, and on eBay, and have tags to say they are authentic métis. The unused ones need a hot wash or two to prepare them, but the used ones have already acquired a lovely, gentle handle. It pays to buy métis from someone you can trust (I got one piece that was so tough it could have been used as a tent or boat's sail) or to touch before you buy. (Look for 'vintage French métis linen sheets' when searching.) It's not the first fabric that springs to mind for quilts, but it's absolutely ideal (see page 14 for some more information).

Working with métis or any fabric that contains linen can be slightly tricky; as soon as you've cut it, the cut edge can begin to go wonky. It's important to keep the edges as straight as possible when cutting – it pays to pull it gently into place along the edge of the quilter's ruler to stop it curving slightly. The tighter the weave, the less movement you will get. This is down-to-earth fabric and pretty sturdy, but it still has a mind of its own.

MATERIALS

Fabric suggestions

For the whites, use any light- to medium-weight household or dress fabrics made from cotton, linen, or a mix of the two. Alternatively, you can now buy some excellent plain quilting cottons that contain linen and therefore have plenty of surface and textural interest. The Robert Kaufman fabrics are particularly good. For the reds, there is a huge choice of quilting cottons, or you can use dress or vintage fabrics.

Quilt top: you will need a total of 200 rectangles 6½ x 3½in (16.5 x 9cm); that is, 100 red and 100 white in multiples of four, so 25 sets of four. You will also need 21in (53.5cm) of fabric 42in (110cm) wide to make the border as shown. Before cutting the fabrics, please see Directions, right, as it is possible to make this quilt using strip piecing rather than individual rectangles. This equates to a total of 1¾yd (1.5m) of red fabric and a total of 1¾yd (1.5m) of white fabric, 21in (53.5cm) of fabric 42in (110cm) wide for the border.

Backing: you will need 3½yd (3.25m) of fabric 42in (110cm) wide, or 72in (183cm) of extra-wide sheeting or métis that is a minimum of 72in (183cm) wide.

Binding: you will need 17½in (44.5cm) of fabric 42in (110cm) wide.

DIRECTIONS

Notes: all seam allowances are ¼in (5mm) unless otherwise stated.

This quilt has five blocks across and five blocks down, so a total of 25 blocks. It could be made smaller or larger by reducing or increasing the number of blocks. Each block is made up of eight rectangles, four red and four white, made into squares that are then machine-pieced to make a large square.

It is not necessary to cut out all the rectangles in one go. You may want to cut out just a few at a time until you are happy that the fabrics are working well together.

Begin by deciding if you are going to cut out the rectangles individually, or if you are going to use the strip-piecing method (see page 96 and below).

1 If cutting out rectangle by rectangle, you will need to cut out a total of 100 red 6½ x 3½in (16.5 x 9cm) rectangles and 100 white 6½ x 3½in (16.5 x 9cm) rectangles.

Working in batches of four matching squares, each made up of one red and one white rectangle, machine-stitch a red rectangle to a white rectangle along one long edge. Iron, pressing the seams to one side, towards the darker colour. Continue until you have 100 two-colour squares in batches of four matching squares per block, enough to make 25 blocks.

2 If you are strip-piecing, cut strips of fabric 3½in (8.5cm) wide and 26in (64cm) long. Machine-piece a strip of red and a strip of white together along one long edge. Iron, pressing the seams to one side, towards the darker colour. Then cut this double-width strip into four 6½in (16cm) squares. This will give you the pieces for one block. Continue in this way until you have 100 squares: enough for 25 blocks.

3 Now, machine-piece the squares together to make the blocks. Bring four matching squares to the sewing machine. Following the illustration (see page 99), machine-piece 1 to 2, then 3 to 4, then sew the 1–2 strip to the 3–4 strip to make a four-square block.

4 Arrange the blocks in five rows of five blocks so that you are happy with the layout. Then machine-piece the blocks together, row by row. Iron each row, pressing the seams to one side. Machine-piece the horizontal rows together to make the top. Iron again, pressing the rows to one side.

5 Make and attach the border. Cut six 3½in (9cm)-wide strips across the full length of 42in (110cm)-wide border fabric (fewer strips if you are using wider fabric). Trim and join them to make one long strip. Machine-sew a length to each short side of the quilt top, then to each long side, cutting the strip and reattaching it to the next side as you work your way round. Press the seam allowances to one side, away from the quilt top. The quilt top is now complete.

6 To make the back, either use a single 72in (183cm) piece of extra-wide métis or sheeting, or make another backing design that is 3–4in (8–10cm) larger all round than the quilt top.

7 Make the quilt sandwich (see page 143 for instructions).

You will also need

A piece of wadding 3–4in (8–10cm) larger all round than the quilt top; I used 100 per cent organic cotton with scrim.
100 per cent cotton all-purpose sewing thread for the machine-piecing and for attaching the binding. Thread for hand-quilting; I recommend cotton perlé 8 for this quilt as this shows up well and comes in a good range of colours. A suitable needle for hand-quilting (I used a sashiko needle).

Finished measurements

66½ x 66½in (169 x 169cm)

8 Hand-quilt the top with a thread of your choice. I used scarlet cotton perlé 8 and made the lines of stitching on the white fabric so that the stitches show up. I stitched rows just outside the vertical seams on the white fabrics and along the horizontal seams. This created a rectangular grid of stitches that shows up clearly on the plain white back.

9 Trim and bind the quilt (see page 146 for instructions).

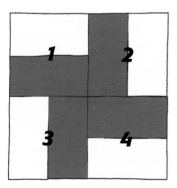

Block illustration: each square block is pieced from four red and four white rectangles.

Layout illustration: the quilt top has five blocks across and five blocks down.

SCOTTISH LOG CABIN

I knew I wanted to make a quilt for this book with a tartan, or similar wool plaid, as it's such a classic style of fabric. I'd seen some amazing tartans containing great colour mixes in projects and garments, but when it came to buying them, I couldn't find anything as bright and unusual as I wanted. I was disappointed, figured I couldn't spend years looking for a dream tartan, and resigned myself to looking for standard tartans containing navy, red, green and white. But then, one time in Joel and Son (www.joelandsonfabrics.com), an amazing fabric shop in London that supplies fabrics to designers, I found this rich, candy pink 'Burberry' check.

I know it's not a true tartan, that it's remarkably similar to one of the most widely copied trademarked designs, and that it's not even authentic Burberry but an Italian lookalike. Nevertheless, the pink, black and café au lait colour combination is a playful modern take on traditional tartan. It's also fantastic-quality 100 per cent wool, with real springiness and beautiful drape, plus it doesn't crease (although this factor and its bounciness are something of a problem when it comes to pressing). It is 60in (150cm) wide, so you get a generous amount if you buy a single metre, which is certainly enough for the jumping-off point for a quilt.

It is such a striking design that it deserves to be the focal point of a quilt, so I decided not to mix it with any more patterns. Instead, I bought a couple of pieces of black silk, going for drama and definition, and an eye-popping, neon-cerise-pink, textured silk, which stood out brilliantly against the black and tartan.

I was happy to use black silk because it's a fabric with a very long history in quilts. It was used a great deal in nineteenth-century American log cabin and courthouse steps quilts, and in English quilts. I would guess that there was plenty left over from mourning dresses and clothes, which would have been made of silk or other light- and medium-weight fabrics, and that patchwork quilters made the most of the availability of black fabric (just think how often it appears in crazy patchwork). It appeared again in quilts made during the Second World War, when most fabrics were in short supply but there were off-cuts of blackout curtain fabric that could be used up. Black silk in particular is a fantastic fabric for quilts (more so than cotton). It has depth and sheen and reflects the light in different ways according to how it is lying; it is also a great contrast to deep and richly coloured fabrics.

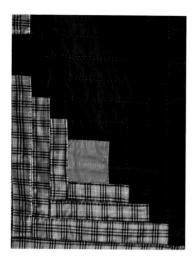

DESIGN

From the moment I unwrapped the check and the silks and found that they were already beginning to fray, I knew it would be best to keep to relatively large, simple pieces and shapes in order to minimise handling and fraying, and I considered making a top with large squares of my fabrics. However, I knew I really wanted to make a log cabin quilt – not with lots of blocks, but as an enormous four-block top that resembles the oversize, single-block quilts made by the quilters of Gee's Bend. This would use wide strips, and show off the tartan to great effect. I was also inspired by the fact that this is a fabric with a Scottish style, and that there are many log cabins and crofts in Scotland, so thought this could be my Scottish Log Cabin quilt, with hot pink central squares rather than the more traditional red 'hearths'.

The blocks

I dithered about cutting into this wonderful tartan-style fabric; every time I touched it I got nervous about misusing it. In the end, I sketched a design before getting out the scissors.

I began by starting in the middle of the quilt and deciding that the central squares would be twice the width of the strips; so the squares would be 6 x 6in (15 x 15cm), finished measurement, and the strips would be 3in (8cm) wide, finished measurement. If you cut thin strips out of a large check or tartan design such as this and sew them back together, it's possible some strips will end up with next to nothing in the way of interest, but a 3in (8cm)-wide strip will always have some check in it and therefore works well. Bigger tartans would need wider strips, and smaller checks would be fine cut into thinner strips. Once you have these starting principles, no further planning is needed, apart from perhaps deciding in advance the number of strips round each square. I didn't know how many times I could go round the square with the fabric I had – one metre of 60in (150cm)-wide fabric and two metres of 45in (112cm)-wide silk; I guessed three or four times when using 3½in (9cm) full-width strips.

I cut out the four central squares, and lots of full-width strips of the check and the silk. I went round each square three times and found I had enough of the check to go round a fourth time without having to make too many strips from leftovers. There is always a possibility that this will happen when making log cabin blocks. Fortunately, I had to resort to making strips from more than one fabric only twice.

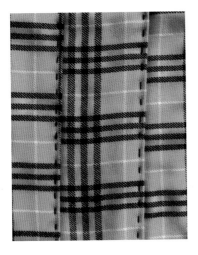

The layout

You have a choice when making the blocks. If you want to have the blocks working as mirror images, you will need to make them following the illustration that shows the way the blocks are built up (see page 105). Or, if you simply want to get results and/or are not sure of the layout before starting, make four standard log cabin blocks and decide how to place them later. I did the latter.

I then made the arrangement I had planned, which was to have the check fabric making a square on point in the middle of the quilt, and the black silk on the outside. This way, I thought, there would be a big, bright expanse of pink 'Burberry' check in the centre. Then my daughter Phoebe suggested that I change them round and put the black in the middle. So I rearranged them. What a revelation. I would have thought that a huge square of black silk would be too dark and dour, but in fact it throws up the hot pink squares by contrast and makes them stand out even more. It is always worth playing with log cabin blocks to discover the best arrangement: it might not be the one you had in mind.

The backing and binding

I went with black edging, which sounds very funereal but turned out to be the right thing. For the back, I used a bright hot pink plain fabric from Robert Kaufman (one of the enormous range of Kona solids that are a gift to quilters). I quilted with cotton perlé 8 – pink on black and black on pink – following the lines of the seams.

MATERIALS

Fabric suggestions

Any very definite check or tartan will work well in this design, and it doesn't have to be wool – cotton checks and plaids would be good. Wool and silk go well together as they both have a richness of texture. If you use cotton checks, a plain cotton (such as Kona) would be a natural partner.

Quilt top: you will need 1 1/4yd (1m) of wool check fabric 60in (150cm) wide, plus 1 3/4yd (1.5m) of silk fabric 45in (112cm) wide, plus four squares of silk 6 1/2 x 6 1/2in (16.5 x 16.5cm).
Backing: you will need 3 1/4yd (3m) of fabric 42in (110cm) wide.
Binding: you will need 15in (38cm) of 42in (110cm) or 45in (112cm)-wide silk.

You will also need

A piece of wadding 3–4in (8–10cm) larger all round than the quilt top; I used 100 per cent organic cotton with scrim.
100 per cent cotton all-purpose sewing thread for the machine-piecing and for attaching the binding. Thread for hand-quilting; I recommend cotton perlé 8 for this quilt as this shows up well and comes in a good range of colours. A suitable needle for hand-quilting (I used a sashiko needle).

Finished measurements

60 x 60in (158 x 158cm)

DIRECTIONS

Notes: Both silk and high-quality, smooth wool fabric are prone to fraying. They require careful, minimal handling. I used 1/4in (5mm) seam allowances, but you could use 1/2in (1cm) allowances if you are worried about your fabric fraying too much. Keep the pieces of fabric large and fold so that the raw edges are covered between sewing times. Trim any bad fraying if necessary, but don't pull loose threads as you may undo more than you bargained for.

There are two ways to make the log cabin blocks. Either make four in the standard way and arrange them as you please. This is easy and gives you flexibility, but you will not have a full mirror-image layout at the end. Or, if you want to be absolutely correct and have mirror images of the blocks, you will need to follow the layout and strip placement as shown in the illustration on page 105. This requires knowing which fabric will go where before you start machine-piecing. It is possible to change the arrangement of the blocks, but if you do, you will not have a mirror-image layout.

1 Cut out the four 6 1/2 x 6 1/2in (16.5 x 16.5cm) central squares.

2 Cut out a few 3 1/2in (9cm) full-width strips of the check and the silk fabrics. Trim the ends. You could cut out all the strips at once if you prefer, but I tend to cut as I go just in case I change my mind or find I have cut out too much.

3 Make four log cabin blocks following one or other of the illustrations on page 105 (see above, and Design, page 102, before deciding how to proceed and before machine-piecing). Cut more strips as you work, and make strips from leftovers if necessary. Aim to use up as many short strips as possible early in the making so that you don't end up having to make long strips out of lots of short strips later. Press the blocks after each round of strips, pressing the seams to one side away from the central square.

4 Press the finished blocks. Arrange and machine-piece the four to make the top. Press again, pressing the seams to one side.

5 Make a backing that is 3–4in (8–10cm) larger all round than the quilt top.

6 Make the quilt sandwich (see page 143 for instructions).

7 Hand-quilt the top with the thread of your choice. I used cotton perlé 8 in bright pink on the black silk, and black on the pink check, stitching just outside the seams to achieve straight lines.

8 Trim and bind the quilt (see page 146 for instructions).

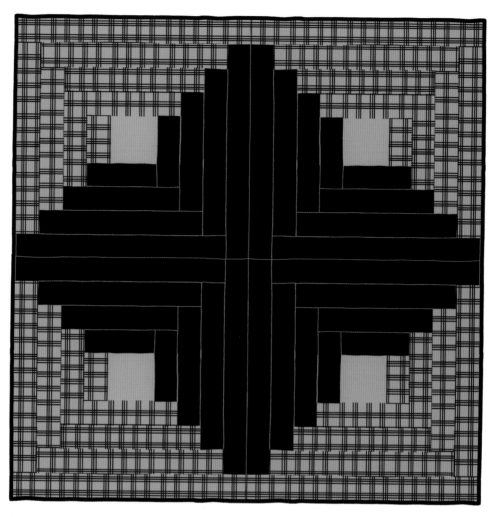

Layout illustration: the quilt has four log cabin blocks that reflect one another.

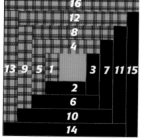

Illustration for top left-hand block.

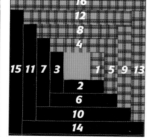

Illustration for top right-hand block.

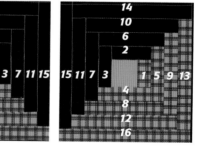

Illustration for bottom left-hand block.

Illustration for bottom right-hand block.

INDIGO BENTO BOX

The world is awash with indigo, but we are all so used to denim jeans that we sometimes forget about the traditional and very beautiful indigo fabrics that are available for projects other than garments. The most alluring are the hand- or yarn-dyed and hand-printed versions made in Japan; these are heirloom, work-of-art fabrics but very expensive. They are made in just two colours, often with a simple, graceful, traditional motif or design, and are ideal for inclusion in quilts – if you can afford them.

However, it's also possible to find cheaper versions in quilting and general fabric shops (and their websites). These are still very distinctive, but because they have been manufactured commercially by machine, they are much more affordable. Makers such as Sevenberry produce very appealing indigo cotton prints, and there are good indigo fabrics from Japan that come without a selvedge (so the exact producer remains anonymous). There are also many equally good indigo fabrics from other parts of the world, such as African batiks and Ikat weaves, that deserve to be put into quilts.

I'd come across a number of the Japanese indigo fabrics without selvedges, with little motifs of flowers and dragonflies, and although I liked their simplicity and colour, I didn't want to make an entirely indigo quilt. Instead, I wanted to lighten and freshen the look by using an ecru-on-indigo print with some indigo-on-ecru fabrics. But when I put my ecru fabric next to the indigo fabrics it looked very dull, as did various off-white/cream quilting cottons with little blue patterns that looked too fussy, and a plain off-white linen that looked too antiseptic and clinical. Eventually, I cut out some squares of the fabric with indigo circles on a white fabric (a Robert Kaufman, 'Metro Living', 'Circles' design) and these worked. It was the whiteness, the simplicity and the graphic repetition of the design that worked, and it demonstrated just how careful you need to be when choosing fabrics to work with indigo.

DESIGN

I'd looked at traditional Japanese quilts in books, such as the excellent *Japanese Quilt Blocks* by Susan Briscoe (A&C Black, 2007) and seen that many contain squares and boxes and are often very geometric and striking. The idea of Japanese boxes made me think of bento boxes, the traditional boxes used for home-packed meals. These are most often square and sometimes are subdivided inside with different square sections holding different foods. As my quilt was made up of squares holding squares, I decided it would be an Indigo Bento Box quilt. It's a version of the Fall Leaves quilt (see page 88) in that it uses five squares to make a cross, but this time the crosses enclose larger squares.

This quilt is quite quick and easy to make once you have decided on the fabrics and the size of the squares. In the finished quilt, the central squares are 6 x 6in (16 x 16cm) and the small indigo squares are 3 x 3in (8 x 8cm).

The fabrics

I used only five indigo designs: I'd planned to use more but one had to be taken out because the non-blue colour was too brown, and one proved to be the wrong shade of blue. Having said that, I did find that a mixture of shades of indigo blue works well (and the colours do vary), but they have to be quite close in shade and depth for the mix to succeed.

Although I had enough fabric to make a single-fabric backing – and the red quilting stands out well on the plain fabric – I broke it up with a strip of one of the indigo fabrics that is used in the top, but placed it slightly higher than midway so that it resembled a kimono sash, which sits above the waist. The binding is red to match the quilting and to create a vivid edge.

The quilting

I used double-thickness Olympus sashiko cotton thread in red, stitched in diagonal lines. I kept to very clear and simple quilting that adds some colour and interest because there is no border (I felt that a border was not necessary as this is a self-contained design already).

MATERIALS

Fabric suggestions

This quilt uses commercially produced indigo fabric from Japan and quilting cottons. It would also work with non-Japanese indigo fabrics such as quilting cottons, African and other batiks, and Ikat weaves.

Quilt top: you will need a total of 2¼yd (2m) of an assortment of 42in (110cm)-wide cotton indigo prints (I used five different designs), plus 1¼yd (1m) of a contrasting fabric for the large squares. (This size quilt uses exactly 1¾yd/1.6m of indigo fabrics, but I always buy a little more to allow for greater flexibility.)

Backing: you will need a total of 2¾yd (2.5m) of fabric 42in (110cm) wide. (See Directions, right, for more information about making the backing as shown.)

Binding: you will need 15in (38cm) of red cotton quilting fabric 42in (110cm) wide.

You will also need

A piece of wadding 3–4in (8–10cm) larger all round than the quilt top; I used 100 per cent organic cotton with scrim.
100 per cent cotton all-purpose sewing thread for the machine-piecing and for attaching the binding.
Thread for hand-quilting; I used two skeins of Olympus red sashiko cotton thread used double. Alternatively, cotton perlé 8 would show up well and comes in a good range of colours.
A suitable needle for hand-quilting (I used a sashiko needle).

Finished measurements
48 x 64in (122 x 162.5cm)

DIRECTIONS

Notes: all seam allowances are ¼in (5mm) unless otherwise stated.

The quilt is made up of five large squares across and seven down. These are surrounded by smaller indigo squares arranged in crosses made up of five squares (see the illustration on page 111 for more information on the layout).

1 To make a quilt this size, you will need to cut a total of 35 central squares 6½ x 6½in (16.5 x 16.5cm), and 212 smaller indigo squares 3¼ x 3¼in (8 x 8cm). It's best to begin by cutting out a few small indigo squares and a couple of large squares to play with possible fabrics. Once you have decided which fabrics work well, you can then cut out all the squares you will need.

2 Arrange the squares according to the layout shown in the illustration, placing the indigo fabric crosses in the positions that work best for the mix of fabrics you are using.

3 Once you are happy with the layout, machine-piece the top. Sew the rows together one by one. The rows with just blue squares are very straightforward. However, with a row that contains the larger contrast squares, it's necessary to machine-piece each of the pairs of indigo squares together before machine-piecing the row; that is to say, machine-piece the sets of two indigo squares to make rectangles, then press, then machine-piece the rectangles to the adjoining squares to make the row. Iron each row, pressing the seams to one side.

4 Now machine-piece the horizontal rows together to make the quilt top. Iron again, pressing the seams to one side.

5 Make a backing that is 3–4in (8–10cm) larger all round than the quilt top. The backing can be plain or you can add a strip or sash. If you add the sash you will need three trimmed pieces to make the back. The backing shown here has a top section 20 x 54in (50 x 137cm), a central sash 9 x 54in (23 x 137cm), and a bottom section 41 x 54in (104 x 137cm). Machine-piece these sections together then iron, pressing the seams open or to one side.

6 Make the quilt sandwich (see page 143 for instructions).

7 Hand-quilt the top with the thread of your choice. I hand-quilted with red sashiko cotton thread used double and a sashiko needle. I stitched a criss-cross grid of lines that run through the corners of the larger squares. I used masking tape as a line guide, carefully lifting it off when each row was finished.

8 Trim and bind the quilt (see page 146 for instructions).

Layout illustration: the back of the quilt has a band of print fabric breaking up a plain fabric.

Layout illustration: the quilt top features crosses made of five small squares, grouped around larger squares.

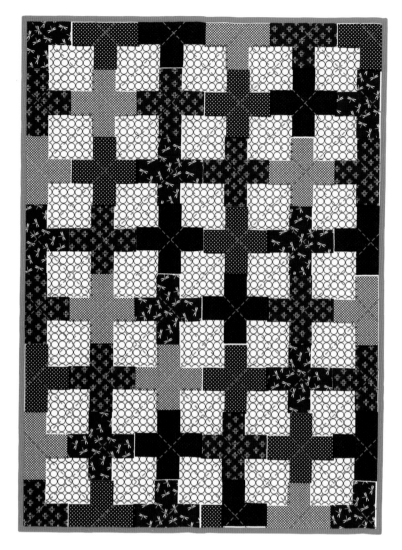

Indigo fabrics

Japanese indigo fabrics are available from quilting suppliers, good fabric shops such as The Cloth House (see Resources, pages 151–153) and specialist fabric websites. Hand-dyed, traditional indigo is beautiful and relatively expensive, but commercially produced versions are also excellent. Manufacturers recommend washing before sewing.

Euro Japan Links (www.eurojapanlinks.com) has a good range of fabrics from Japan.

Clothaholics (http://clothaholics.com) sells beautiful, authentic Japanese hand-dyed fabrics.

Sashiko threads and needles are available from The Cotton Patch (see Resources, page 152).

HARRIS TWEED

This is a Harris Tweed story, plain and simple. It's such an iconic fabric that I wanted to try it out in a quilt, and I was delighted with the result; so much so that I made a second version. The first is designed around a single piece of wide-width Harris Tweed, while the second uses off-cuts and scraps mixed with the types of fabrics you might easily find in your wardrobe.

There are many types of tweed (see pages 15–16), but only one Harris Tweed with the Orb Mark, the certification mark that confirms that a fabric complies with all the necessary regulations. To be stamped 'Harris Tweed', it must be made from 100 per cent wool that has been dyed, spun and finished in the Outer Hebrides, and hand-woven by the islanders in their own homes 'in the islands of Lewis, Harris, Uist and Barra and their several purtenances'.

The wool itself comes mostly from mainland Scotland, but the island communities also add their local wool to the clip. The wool is dyed, spun and warped, and delivered with the weft yarn to the homes of each weaver, who hand-weaves the required pattern on his or her home loom. The fabric is then returned to the manufacturers for finishing and quality control. It is the very traditional production method, the fact that the fabric is made by craftspeople, the quality, and the wonderful colours that all make Harris Tweed so special. It offers weight and warmth and great protection from the elements, and although it's been through difficult times due to changing tastes in fashion, there is always a market for this tough, hardwearing, unique tweed.

Every piece of Harris Tweed (which is woven in 54½yd/50m lengths) has its own characteristics. Some are simply flecked or lightly striped; some contain very subtle shades; and some have more striking patterns and colours. It is a fabric that requires you to look closely in order to see and appreciate the cleverness of the weave, and quilting is a great opportunity to get very close to this amazing fabric.

WARP AND WEFT

I came across a 1¼yd (1m) piece of 60in (150cm)-wide Harris tweed, which I loved because the colours and pattern were classic but also a little unusual. You don't always find burnt orange and emerald green in Harris tweed, but these work beautifully in a simple check together with chestnut brown, all on a plain light brown background.

As it was the colour combination that had caught my eye, I wanted to pick out similarly rich colours to work with the tweed. I found a Philip Jacobs 'Variegated Leaves' design that works well (it's a very unorthodox geranium print in greens, golds and browns), then added an old-gold velvet, a very dark brown velvet from an old skirt, a brilliant emerald green corduroy that was also from a skirt, a white-on-emerald spot quilting cotton from Lecien, and a charming green and white graphic print, which is 'Lily' by Alice Kennedy for Timeless Treasures (this last also appears on the binding).

I didn't need any more fabrics than these, and although I didn't have very much of some of them (the velvets in particular), I managed to come up with a design that worked and allowed me to use what I had. The quilt is really a showcase for the Harris tweed, and everything else is there to highlight its clever design, colours and beautiful quality.

The backing picks out the warm gold feel in the tweed. It's a deep yellow Metro Living 'Circles' design from Robert Kaufman.

DESIGN

I wanted a design that would evoke the idea of a warp and a weft, of yarns going under and over each other, and I also wanted to echo the small check pattern in the tweed fabric itself. I debated the size of the squares, and initially thought big. However, smaller proved to be the better option and allowed me to get more out of the fabrics in short supply (the brown velvet and the emerald cord). Once I had decided on the basic layout, it was easy to build up the quilt using lots of tweed squares and lines of contrasting fabrics.

The border and the stitching

I framed the central 'warp and weft' section with a dark border of velvet and a second border of the geranium print, and used up all the remaining tweed in a nicely deep outer border that allows the fabric to be seen and shown off over a larger area. I hand-quilted with emerald green cotton perlé 8 thread, making a grid of lines that run through the middle of the squares to create a further Scottish plaid/tartan effect.

The layout

The basic layout could be extended, and the 'warp and weft' section could cover the entire top. This is a very flexible quilt design that can be adapted to suit the fabrics you have at your disposal.

MATERIALS

Fabric suggestions

Tweed, wool check or tartan for the main fabric, plus a variety of fabrics such as cord, velvet, satin, silk, cotton for the contrast squares and borders.

Quilt top: 1¼yd (1m) of wool or tweed fabric 60in (150cm) wide (this is enough for the squares and the border), plus a total of 24in (61cm) of a variety of fabrics 42in (110cm) wide for the contrast squares (or the equivalent if using wider fabrics), plus 12½in (31.75cm) each of two fabrics 42in (110cm) wide for the two inner borders (or the equivalent if using wider fabrics). Alternatively, if you are working on a more flexible basis, allow for 1¼yd (1m) of tweed fabric, plus a grand total of 1¾yd (1.5m) of an assortment of contrasting fabrics.
Backing: you will need 2¾yd (2.5m) fabric 42in (110cm) wide.
Binding: you will need 15in (38cm) of fabric 42in (110cm) wide.

You will also need

A piece of wadding 3–4in (8–10cm) larger all round than the quilt top; I used 100 per cent organic cotton with scrim.
100 per cent cotton all-purpose sewing thread for the machine-piecing and for attaching the binding. Thread for hand-quilting, such as 100 per cent cotton quilting thread, or cotton perlé 8, or three to six strands of stranded cotton embroidery thread (I used cotton perlé 8 in emerald green). A suitable needle for hand-quilting (I used a sashiko needle).

Finished measurements

58 x 49in (147.5 x 124.5cm)

DIRECTIONS

Notes: all seam allowances are ¼in (5mm) unless otherwise stated.

If you know which fabrics you are using, it's possible to cut out all the pieces in advance. If you are not sure what will work and what won't, cut out just a few squares of each possible fabric and experiment with them first before deciding (see the illustration on page 117 to see how the squares have been laid out).

1 Make the central 'warp and weft' section first. Cut out 91 squares of tweed 3 x 3in (8 x 8cm). Cut out 91 squares of contrasting fabrics 3 x 3in (8 x 8cm) in multiples of six and seven. You will need seven sets of six squares and seven sets of seven squares to make up the rows.

2 Lay out the squares so that there are horizontal rows of contrasting fabrics (see illustration on page 117). When you are happy with the arrangement, machine-piece the rows together one by one. Take care to handle the tweed fabric carefully to reduce the amount of fraying. Iron each row very gently, pressing the seams to one side or open, as you prefer.

3 Now machine-piece the rows together to make the central section. Iron again very gently, pressing the seams to one side or open, as you prefer.

4 For the inner border, cut four 2½in (6cm)-wide strips across the full width of the fabric. Trim the ends and sew them together to make a longer strip. Press the seam allowances open. Machine-sew a length to each short side of the warp and weft section, then to each long side, cutting the strip and reattaching it to the next side as you work your way round. You may need to cut an extra 2½in (6cm)-wide piece to lengthen the strip to go all the way round if your border runs out. Gently press the seam allowances to one side, facing away from the warp and weft section.

5 For the middle border, cut five 2½in (6cm) strips across the full width of your fabric (four strips if you are using 60in/150cm-wide fabric, such as velvet). Trim the ends and sew them together to make a longer strip, then press the seam allowances open. Attach the strip to the edges of the inner border in the same way that the border was attached to the warp and weft section. Press the seam allowances away from the inner border.

6 For the outer border, cut four strips 4½in (11.5cm) wide across the full width of the 60in (150cm)-wide tweed fabric (cut five if you are using a fabric 42in/110cm wide). Join the strips and attach them to the edges of the second border as before, pressing the seams away from that border.

7 Make a backing that is 3–4in (8–10cm) larger all round than the quilt top.

8 Make the quilt sandwich (see page 143 for instructions).

9 Hand-quilt the top with the thread of your choice. Make rows of running stitch to create a grid: I stitched lines running through the middle of each square so that they intersect in the centre, but it could be a criss-cross grid. If you use masking tape as line guides, as I do, be very careful when pulling it off the quilt top to avoid damaging the fabrics.

10 Trim and bind the quilt (see page 146 for instructions).

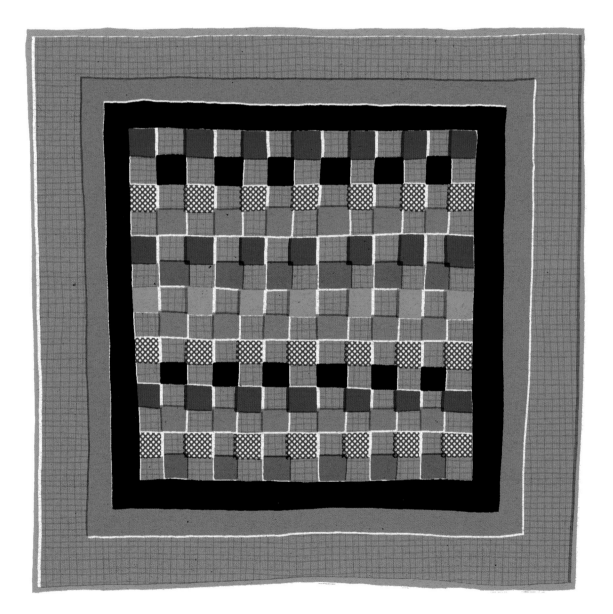

Layout illustration: the quilt top has a central section of 13 squares across and 14 squares down, surrounded by three borders.

WARDROBE

If you can't get hold of a large single piece of Harris tweed (or similar tweed), the Wardrobe quilt is a way to make a tweedy quilt using smaller pieces of tweed salvaged from garments or collected as small off-cuts. As it's not always easy to find enough tweed this way to make a whole quilt, I have supplemented the tweeds with other fabrics from the wardrobe, such as velvet, corduroy, wool suiting, shirting and dress cottons. There is nothing in this quilt top that can't be cut from a jacket, skirt, shirt or pair of trousers.

I started with a bag of off-cuts of Harris tweed bought on eBay because I was fascinated by the variety of patterns and colours. But I also like the way that Harris tweed (and other tweeds) work so well with many other fabrics that you'd find in your wardrobe, particularly the other hearty, wintry, cosy, sturdy, practical fabrics such as corduroy and velvet. It also works brilliantly with lighter fabrics such as shirt and dress cottons, and looks lovely with classic Liberty Tana lawn designs.

When I got out the pieces of tweed and sorted out the ones that worked well together, I saw I had the beginnings of a rather peaty, heathery palette with small highlights of turquoise, emerald green, black-and-white houndstooth check, and a red and blue check on white. I added small amounts of bright lemon-lime jumbo cord, and several longer strips of dark velvet and brown jumbo cord.

DESIGN

As I wanted to get as much tweed into the quilt top as possible, I began by cutting out the longest, widest pieces I could, and then added the other fabrics cut to the same width, but in different lengths. This is a quite unplanned quilt that grew organically and according to what I had to work with. In this way, I built up a series of strips of varying widths, and ended up with ten strips across made up of five to eight fabrics.

The backing

I wanted the backing to be made out of Viyella, a fabric I grew up with and that I always associate with men's shirts worn under tweed jackets. It is a beautifully soft wool/cotton mix, usually with an off-white background and a simple square check made up of two colours. I looked around for some but couldn't find any (I'm not sure it's made any more). Instead, I used a cotton shirting with the woven pattern closest to Viyella that I could find. The binding is a fine brown needlecord taken from a pair of trousers.

The quilting

I hand-quilted the top with a turquoise cotton perlé 8 thread, making a row of running stitch just inside the left-hand vertical seam of each strip. I chose turquoise so that it would stand out and because it picks up the small splashes of turquoise tweed scattered over the quilt top.

MATERIALS

Fabric suggestions

This quilt was made with scraps and off-cuts; the finished size was determined by the availability of the fabrics. I would not advise trying to replicate this design exactly, but use it as a starting point and as a way of using up and showing off any lovely fabrics you have. It's more a design idea than an exact template, and can be adapted in many ways.

Quilt top: you will need a total of 2¾yd (2.5m) of pieces of fabric in a mix of tweed, corduroy, velvet, woven wool checks and plaids.
Backing: you will need enough fabric to make a backing that is 3–4in (8–10cm) larger all round than the quilt top. If you are using 60in (150cm)-wide shirting you will need 2yd (1.75m). If you are using 42in (110cm) cotton quilting fabric you will need 2¾yd (2.5m).
Binding: you will need 15in (38cm) of fabric 42in (110cm) wide.

You will also need

A piece of wadding 3–4in (8–10cm) larger all round than the quilt top; I used 100 per cent organic cotton with scrim.
100 per cent cotton all-purpose sewing thread for the machine-piecing and for attaching the binding. Thread for hand-quilting, such as 100 per cent cotton quilting thread, or cotton perlé 8, or three to six strands of stranded cotton embroidery thread. I used cotton perlé 8 in turquoise. A suitable needle for hand-quilting (I used a sashiko needle).

Finished measurements
50 x 61in (127 x 155cm)

DIRECTIONS

Notes: all seam allowances are ¼in (5mm) unless otherwise stated.

The quilt is made up of a series of strips that vary in width and the number of fabric sections according to the maximum size piece I could get from the Harris tweed off-cuts and the garments I was cutting up to use. Both the width and length of the strips and pieces within the strips can be altered to suit the fabrics you have. As a result the directions below are a set of guidelines for making this sort of strippy quilt with recycled fabrics and oddments.

1 Sort out the fabrics you plan to use. Wash and iron if necessary. Select the largest pieces first and trim to the maximum size rectangle or strip possible, making sure the width is sensible (half inch/inch or a whole centimetre, depending on your preferred measurement system) so that it's easy to cut more fabrics to match. Cut more, smaller pieces of the same width from different fabrics in order to create long strips. The strips in this quilt are all between 4½in (11.5cm) and 6½in (16.5cm) wide before sewing. The long strips of tweed are all between 29in (73.5cm) and 7in (18cm) long. The smaller pieces of contrasting fabric are all between 4in (10cm) and 2½in (6cm) long before sewing.

2 Using the illustration (see page 121) as a guide, lay out the pieces before sewing them. Break up the pieces of tweed with bright contrasting fabrics, and aim to have a balanced spread of the different fabrics and various widths. My quilt is made up of ten strips altogether.

3 When you are happy with the layout, machine-piece one vertical strip at a time, ironing each one afterwards and pressing the seams to one side. Continue in this way to make all the strips. Do not worry if the strips are not all the same length as the top can be trimmed later.

4 Machine-piece the strips together to make the quilt top. Begin each row of stitching at the end where the previous seam finished, so that in effect you are making a U-turn at the end of each line of stitching. (If you begin the stitching at the same end every time, the quilt top will become distorted.) Mark the end of each seam with a pin if you are likely to forget which direction to sew the next seam in. Iron the top, pressing the seams to one side. Trim the top and bottom edges to straighten if necessary.

5 Now make the backing. If you have a fabric that is wider than the top (such as shirting), this is very easy as all you have to do is cut a length 4–6in (10–15cm) longer than the top. If not, piece together the fabric/s you do have to make a backing that is 3–4in (8–10cm) larger all round than the quilt top.

6 Make the quilt sandwich (see page 143 for instructions).

7 Hand-quilt the top with the thread of your choice. I used cotton perlé 8 in turquoise and stitched just inside the left-hand seam on each row, so that there are long vertical lines of running stitch.

8 Trim and bind the quilt (see page 146 for instructions).

*Layout illustration: the quilt top has ten strips across, each
pieced from a variety of fabrics.*

DECKCHAIR STRIPES

Although there are such things as sober stripes – like those on pinstriped suits and regimental ties – it's the jaunty, cheerful types of stripes that inspire me, the kind that you find on seaside rock and candy, Breton sweaters, barber shops, toothpaste, circus tents and clowns' outfits, rainbows, shirts, rugby tops, and less conformist ties.

I like stripes that have an element of the seaside about them, a holiday feel. Think of deckchairs, windbreaks, towels and swimming costumes, awnings and beach huts, marquees and helter skelters, all with an exuberance that comes from putting clashing and bright colours next to each other, and ignoring anything too controlled, tasteful or subtle.

I particularly enjoy seeing rows of red and white or blue and white or green and white deckchairs on the beach or in parks, but even stripy deckchairs don't have to stop at two colours, as I realised when I discovered the very colourful Deckchair Stripes website (www.deckchairstripes.com). This is a company dedicated to stripes, and it has an amazing selection of interior and deckchair stripes that they also use to make other items such as aprons. When I first saw the website I wanted a bit of every fabric – I found it very difficult to choose just one stripe – so I was delighted when I saw that it is possible to buy sample swatch bags that contain dozens of strips and off-cuts packaged in little drawstring cotton bags.

As soon as the first bag arrived, I got out all the fabrics, lined them up to get a full-on stripy effect for fun, saw they looked amazing, but didn't even consider using them to making a quilt as at that point I was still not thinking outside the realm of lightweight cottons for my quilts. Even when I posted a photo of the lined-up strips on my blog and said it was great quilt inspiration, I didn't make the connection. It was only when I was planning the contents of this book that I realised there was a stripy quilt just asking to be made from deckchair fabric.

DESIGN

I bought more swatch bags (I used three in total, as some strips were too thin or short to be useful – although the majority are very generous and long). I tipped out the contents of all three bags, and worked my way through the strips, laying them out pretty much in the way they had come out of the bags. I made five horizontal rows with the pieces and stood back. It was amazing that without any planning or forethought, I'd made a quilt top in a matter of minutes – all because the sample bags had such a huge range of stripes. I then scrutinised the layout more carefully, saw where a few stripes weren't working too well (for example, ones that were too similar to neighbours, too pale or too dark), or where they pooled a little to make dark or light patches. And that was my quilt top design sorted.

The strips

I trimmed every single strip to straighten the sides. I didn't cut the strips to any specific size and there was no planning with regard to widths. Once I had trimmed the strips to go in the top row, I re-lined them up in order and worked out the optimum length of the pieces. This turned out to be 14in (35.5cm). I then trimmed each strip in each row to that length – this was undoubtedly the most time-consuming aspect of making this particular quilt.

Because of the way it is woven, deckchair canvas – or any similar sturdy, tough fabric – has very little stretch or 'give'. This means you have to cut accurately as there is no possibility of easing the fabric to fit and making ends meet. This is a very straightforward fabric to machine-sew, and doesn't fray. However, it is worth reversing at the beginning and end of every section of sewing to ensure the stitches don't come undone. This isn't necessary with lightweight cottons, but canvas is such a strong fabric that even ironing it can cause the stitches to start to pull away.

Once I had the layout, it was just a matter of sewing together the strips to make the rows, and putting together the five rows to make the top.

The backing

Although there are many good striped quilting cottons available, this was a good chance to use 56in (140cm)-wide shirting cotton in a very jaunty royal blue and white stripe. It has the advantage of being much wider than quilting cotton, which means the backing can be made from a single piece. The same fabric was also used for the binding, which was cut so that I had short stripes going all round the outside of the quilt.

The tying

Unless you have very strong hands and tough fingers or are very determined, canvas is too tough to hand-quilt, so tying works well. This quilt is hand-tied with the knots showing on the back rather than the front where they would distract from the stripiness. Tying is quick and easy (see page 144), and the knots can be placed wherever you like. I put them at the corners of the strips, but they could equally well be placed within the strips. I used several shades of lilac and purple cotton perlé 8, used double, and left relatively long loose ends.

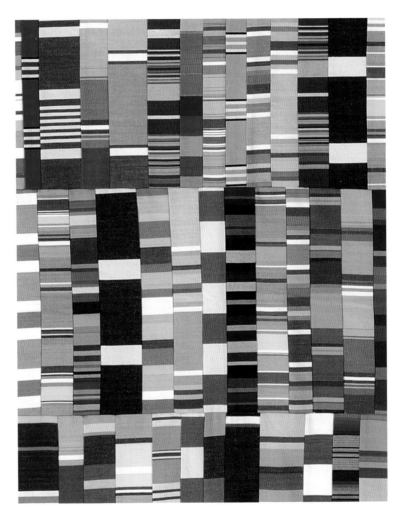

Section of quilt front.

MATERIALS

Fabric suggestions

Almost any type of striped fabric can be used. Ticking, upholstery fabric and shirting are all worth considering. If you prefer to work with something light and easy, there are plenty of striped quilting cottons available. eQuilter (www.equilter.com) has a vast selection of bright and breezy stripes.

This particular quilt is made from fabrics from Deckchair Stripes (www.deckchairstripes.com), which sells bags of strips.

Quilt top: you will need a total of 2yd (1.75m) of striped fabric 56–60in (140–150cm) wide, or 2¾yd (2.5m) of striped fabric 42in (110cm) wide, in as big a mix of colours as possible. Alternatively, use three bags of sample swatches (buy the 'all fabrics' bags) from Deckchair Stripes.
Backing: you will need 75in (190cm) of cotton shirting 56in (140cm) wide, or 2¾yd (2.5m) of fabric 42in (110cm) wide.
Binding: you will need 10in (25cm) of cotton shirting 56in (140cm) wide, or 15in (38cm) of fabric 42in (110cm) wide.

You will also need

A piece of wadding 3–4in (8–10cm) larger all round than the quilt top; I used 100 per cent organic cotton with scrim.
100 per cent cotton all-purpose sewing thread for the machine-piecing and for attaching the binding.
Thread for tying, or cotton perlé 5 (or 8 used double), or six-strand cotton embroidery thread (I used cotton perlé 8).
A suitable needle (I used a sashiko needle).

Finished measurements

46 x 66½in (117 x 169cm)

DIRECTIONS

Note: all seam allowances are ¼in (5mm) unless otherwise stated.

1 If you are using a Deckchair Stripes bag of off-cuts, begin by laying out the strips in as random or as planned a manner as you please. There are so many different stripes in the bags that it's difficult to impose any plan. It may be easier just to lay out the fabrics as they emerge from the bag, then do some adjusting to the overall look. Omit any very thin or very short strips. The minimum useful width is about 1½in (4cm); the minimum useful length is 15in (38cm).

2 Make five horizontal rows of strips, each row approximately 55in (130cm) wide (before sewing). Each row will contain an average of 26 thin vertical strips. First, trim the long sides of each strip to the maximum useful width. Then work out the length they need to be trimmed to, and trim them so they are all the same length. This will depend on the maximum length you can obtain from your set of strips without having to remove too many shorter strips. In the quilt shown, the strips are 14in (35.5cm) long before sewing.

3 If you are using non-deckchair fabrics that do not come as strips and need to be cut into strips, begin by deciding on the length of your strips. The deckchair canvas stripe quilt uses 14in (35.5cm) long strips (before sewing), but the strips could be shorter or longer depending on your taste. Cut strips that vary in width from 1½–3½in (4–9cm) wide in a variety of different fabrics. Lay these out as you please – there is no set pattern or repeat in this quilt. Make five rows of strips, each row approximately 55in (130cm) wide, or make wider or more rows if desired, and if you have sufficient fabric.

4 Starting at the top left-hand corner of the laid-out quilt, machine-piece the strips together to make the rows. Begin each row of stitching at the end where the previous seam finished, so that in effect you are making a U-turn at the end of each line of stitching. (If you begin the stitching at the same side every time, the row will become distorted.) Mark the end of each seam with a pin if you are likely to forget which direction to sew the next seam in. Press the seam allowances to one side, alternating the direction of pressing with each row.

5 Machine-piece the rows together to make the quilt top. Iron it again, pressing the seams to one side.

6 If you are using backing fabric that is wider than the quilt top (such as shirting fabric), you can now make a backing with a single piece of fabric. If you are using fabric that is narrower than the back, piece sections or widths together to make the back. Either way, ensure the backing is 3–4in (8–10cm) larger all round than the top.

7 Make the quilt sandwich (see page 143 for instructions).

8 Machine-quilt, hand-quilt (if you are made of stern stuff), or hand-tie the top (see page 144). I hand-tied this quilt with several shades of lilac and purple cotton perlé 8 thread, used double.

9 Trim and bind the quilt (see page 146 for instructions).

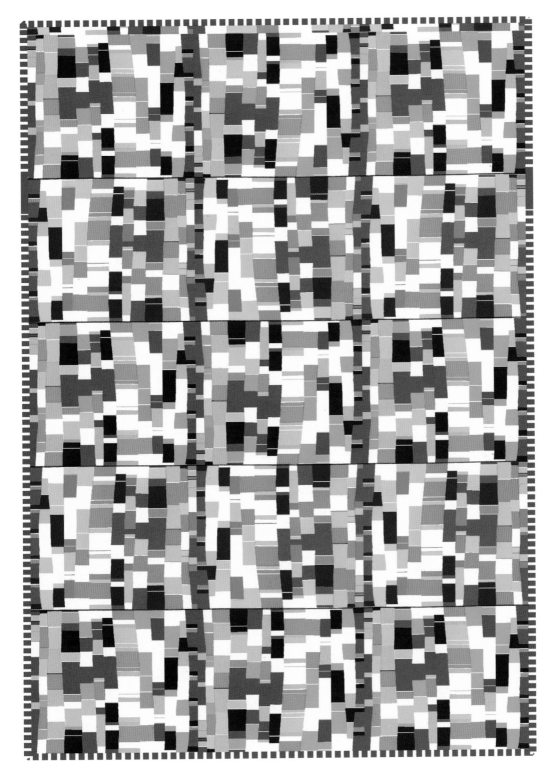

*Layout illustration: the quilt top has five horizontal rows,
each composed of about 26 vertical strips.*

HARLEQUIN

The Harlequin quilt is an ode to velvet. I have loved velvet for as long as I can remember; it's one of those fabrics that thrilled me as a child, and I have never stopped loving its wonderful texture, beautiful handle and drape, and the way it makes any colour look beautiful. I particularly adore the plush, matt, firm cotton velvets that come in so many colours – the type that has a short, smooth pile and a lovely depth of colour.

I put velvet into other quilts in this book (see Warp and Weft quilt, page 114), but also wanted to make a quilt top solely out of velvet – nothing else, just velvet. I thought of strips and squares, but was not convinced these shapes would work well (they could end up looking a little dull). In the end I decided on equilateral triangles, which then came to look like diamonds because of the way I arranged the colours. The pointy diamond effect makes me think of Harlequin outfits in the theatre, which stand out by dint of their rich, bright colours and striking design. Diamonds work brilliantly with solid colours because the repetition of the shape creates all the extra interest, playfulness and eye-catching effects you need.

However, at the point when I was buying the fabrics for the quilt, I was still stuck for a design idea, and simply bought a number of 10in (25cm) lengths in a range of colours. The colours could be any selection you like, but I chose rich, classic, 'stately home' shades in a mix of dark and light tones (not super-brights, and not too many primary colours). A Harlequin quilt could be made out of two colours and would look glorious, or you can use as many as you like. I included fourteen or fifteen colours as I had a few spare pieces left over from other projects. I was surprised by how this design can swallow up colours and still keep its identity.

All the velvets in this quilt are 100 per cent cotton, and some are thicker than others (that is, upholstery-weight). I would have liked to make a silk velvet quilt but two things prevented me: cost, and the fact that silk velvet is very difficult to work with. I found cotton velvet tricky enough, but silk velvet is terribly slippy and I know I would have given up, even if I could have afforded the fabric.

Cotton velvet requires careful and swift handling; it often pays to pin the right sides together before machine-piecing to prevent it slipping out of place, and to use both hands when sewing – one to feed the fabric under the needle and one on the other side to guide it gently through. It frays very quickly; I find it best to leave the loose strands until I've finished the project and to cut them all at the end; if I trim as I go along, this leads to more fraying and more loss of fabric.

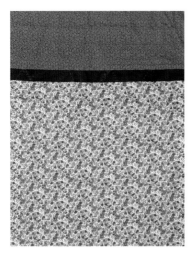

DESIGN

I had my bright idea for a triangle design, but was then amazed at how hard it is to create an equilateral triangle template, especially when it's one that is much bigger than the usual, and you don't have enlarging facilities on a copier at home. I wanted to use an exaggeratedly large triangle because velvet is not the easiest fabric to work with, and I thought it would be better to use fewer but bigger pieces and create a theatrical effect, but I found it was impossible to find any decent-size triangle template. In the end, I made my own out of cardboard to use as a placing guide, but used the 60-degree line on my quilter's ruler to get the angles and lines correct when cutting.

I based the design on an equilateral triangle (one in which all three sides and angles are the same) that was 8in (20cm) high when cut out, with a 60-degree angle in each corner. When cutting the triangles from the fabric, it's necessary to cut out a strip that is ¾in (2cm) wider/taller than the chosen height of the triangle, so I used 8¾in (22cm) strips. The design also requires 16 half-triangles, one for either end of each row.

I cut out a number of equilateral triangles, still without a set plan, and arranged them in several ways, until I saw that they could be divided, quite loosely, into dark and light. They could then be set out to create two-colour diamonds in a light/dark pattern that is eye-catching and dramatic. I then added the half- triangles to the ends of each row and machine-pieced the top row by row.

I left the quilt without a border because I like the simple, large diamonds and felt they didn't need any framing. I hand-quilted with cotton perlé 8 thread, stitching just inside the seams of the diamonds.

The backing and binding

The quilt is backed with several fabrics. I very much like the look of Liberty Tana Lawn and velvet together (they are both timeless classics), so used a piece of lawn that picks out many of the colours in the top. As this wasn't large enough for the whole back, I added a mid-blue cotton quilting fabric and a strip of blue velvet between the cotton and the lawn – which reminds me of little girls' dresses made out of pretty floral fabric with a velvet sash.

The binding is a two-colour indigo-blue cotton quilting print that picks out two of blue velvets in the top. I hand-quilted the top just inside the seams of the diamonds with cotton perlé 8 thread in a rich, old-gold colour.

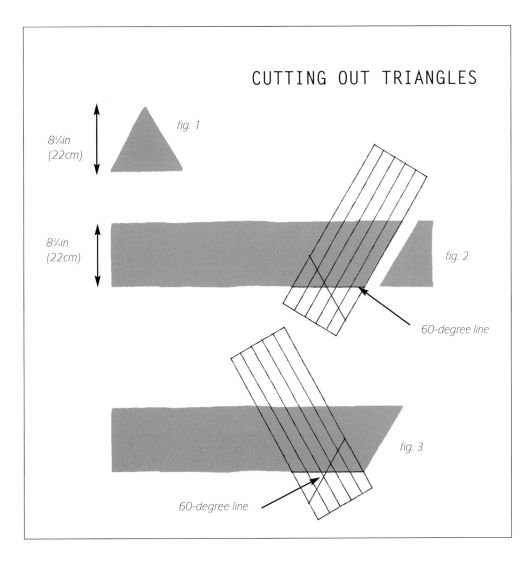

CUTTING OUT TRIANGLES

8¾in
(22cm)

fig. 1

8¾in
(22cm)

fig. 2

60-degree line

fig. 3

60-degree line

To cut out triangles (fig. 1):
1. Cut an 8¾in (22cm)-wide strip of velvet across the width of the fabric
(selvedge to selvedge).
2. Align the 60-degree line of your quilter's ruler with the long edge
of the fabric strip (fig. 2).
3. Cut along the right edge of the ruler to establish the first edge
of the triangle. (You will not need the end piece.)
4. Rotate the ruler, aligning its other 60-degree line along the bottom
edge of the strip. The edge of the ruler should be positioned to form
a point at the bottom edge of your first cut (fig. 3).
5. Cut along the right side of the ruler to create a triangle
6. Continue flipping your ruler from side to side to cut more equilateral
triangles.
7. To make the two half-triangles for the beginning and end of each
row, simply cut a full triangle in two down the central line of symmetry –
that is, from the centre of the base line to the apex/point above.

MATERIALS

Fabric suggestions

See page 17 for advice on choosing and working with velvet before buying and cutting out. Medium-weight cotton velvet in solid colours, or fine/medium corduroy would work well, as would solid-colour or tweedy woven wool fabrics. Alternatively, apply the design to solid cottons and linens.

Quilt top: if using a 60in (150cm)-wide cotton velvet, you will need a total of 2yd (1.75m). You need 1yd (90cm) in light colours and 1yd (90cm) in dark colours, e.g. four of each. If you are using 42in (110cm)-wide fabric, you will need 2¾yd (2.5m) in a mix of colours, dark and light 42in (110cm)-wide fabric. Half should be light colours, and half should be dark colours, e.g. four to six of each.

Backing: you will need a total of 2¾yd (2.5m) of fabric 42in (110cm) wide.

Binding: you will need 15in (38cm) of fabric 42in (110cm) wide.

You will also need

A piece of wadding 3–4in (8–10cm) larger all round than the quilt top; I recommend 100 per cent organic cotton with scrim.
100 per cent cotton all-purpose sewing thread in ecru or taupe for the machine-piecing and for hand-finishing the binding.
Thread for quilting, such as 100 per cent cotton quilting thread, cotton perlé 8, or three to six strands of stranded cotton embroidery thread for hand-quilting. I used cotton perlé 8 and a sashiko needle.

Finished measurements

45½ x 70in (115 x 178cm)

DIRECTIONS

Notes: All seam allowances are ¼in (5mm) unless otherwise stated.

This quilt is made with equilateral triangles; i.e. triangles that are the same length on each side, with 60-degree angles at each of the three corners. The finished triangles are 8in (20cm) high from the centre of the base line to the apex. It may help to make a template out of cardboard first. This can then be placed on the fabric to make it easier to position the ruler. As you must add ¾in (2cm) to the finished height of the triangle before cutting, you need to ensure the template triangle is 8¾in (22cm) high from the centre of the base line to the apex – see illustration on page 131.
It is also possible to cut out the triangles without a template, simply using the angle markings on a quilter's ruler (see illustrations with ruler on page 131).

1 If you are following the design as shown, please refer to the illustration for the layout on page 133. Cut out forty dark equilateral triangles and forty light equilateral triangles. Cut eight of the light triangles in half to make the sixteen light half triangles which are placed at either end of each row.

2 Lay out the triangles using the illustration as your guide, or create your own pattern. When you are happy with the layout, join each row of triangles together working from left to right to create a strip. Press the seams to one side, alternating the direction of pressing with each row.

3 Join the rows of triangles together to create the top. Press the seams to one side.

4 Now make the back so that it is 3–4in (8–10cm) larger all round than the top. You can either use one single-width fabric or a number of sections machine-pieced together.

5 Make the quilt sandwich (see page 143 for instructions).

6 Hand-quilt with the thread of your choice, following seams as line guides.

7 Trim and bind the quilt (see page 146 for instructions).

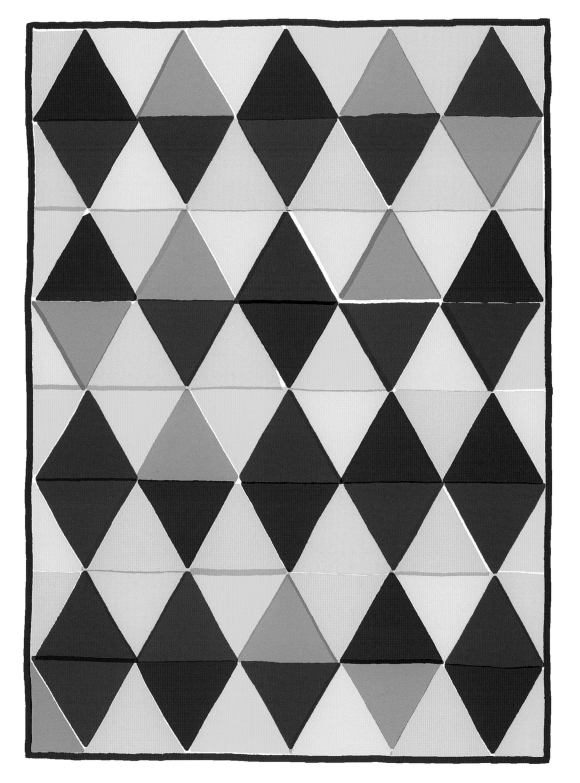

*Layout illustration: the quilt top is made from triangles
pieced to form a pattern of pale and dark diamonds.*

MAKING QUILTS

It's very easy to rush headlong into quilting and to get caught up in a whirlwind of cutting, only to realise the fabrics aren't working and you've gone too fast for your own good. On the other hand, for many people, it's just as easy to feel paralysed by the challenge of translating inspiration and a pile of fabrics into a finished quilt. So it helps, in both cases, to take a deep breath and to take quilt-making one step at a time.

I was very apprehensive when I first started quilting, until I took a weekend patchwork and quilting course and learned the basic skills of using a rotary cutter, a self-healing mat and a quilter's ruler, and discovered that these were all I needed in order to make the sorts of quilts I wanted to make (the sort you see here in this book). There are plenty more techniques I could, and may yet, acquire, but I found that once I was confident with cutting and handling fabric, I could deal with the elements of making a quilt in a step-by-step fashion, allowing it to develop organically, rather than sticking doggedly to a vision of what I was aiming to achieve. The more quilts I made, the more I broke down quilt-making into a series of decisions; something that makes the whole process far more enjoyable and far less nerve-racking.

In this section you will find my thoughts on making quilts and basic directions for the methods that I have developed over time. Of course, there are all sorts of ways to make quilts, and you may find that my approach is quite different to that of other books and quilters. But it has been tried and tested at home, and is rooted in the firm conviction that making quilts should be manageable, straightforward and enjoyable rather than a matter of following a set of rigid rules. As a result, I have discarded some of the accepted wisdom and techniques, and simplified the process as much as possible. You will find here what I hope are useful, down-to-earth, pragmatic ideas for making machine-pieced and hand-quilted quilts.

WHAT YOU NEED

First, a checklist of the essential equipment that is needed to make simple but beautiful quilts. This is what you will need in addition to your fabrics and filling.

❖ A rotary cutter (and a spare blade) for cutting out quilt pieces: the two best-known brands are Fiskars and Olfa, and both are excellent. Handle and use with care as the blades are lethally sharp.

❖ A self-healing mat (the largest you can afford and store): the one I use is 24 x 35in (60 x 90cm). For a long time I used a 17 x 23in (43 x 58cm) mat that was fine, but I find that anything smaller can make it difficult to cut out large pieces.

❖ Two or three quilter's rulers. It's not necessary to have many; a long rectangle and a large square will be enough for almost all projects. Brand-wise, I use Creative Grids rulers because they have a very useful half-inch edge (instead of measuring only in full inches), which makes cutting with the seam allowance very easy. I use just three rulers: a large square 15½ x 15½in (40 x 40cm); a smaller square 10½ x 10½in (26.5 x 26.5cm), and a long rectangle 7½ x 23½in (19 x 60cm).

❖ A sewing machine that is reliable, can sew a straight line and go forwards and backwards – nothing fancier is needed for this sort of quilting. The presser foot should measure ¼in (5mm) from the needle to the outside edge so that you can use this as your guide when sewing ¼in (5mm) seams. My machine is a basic but sturdy second-hand 25-year-old Bernina Nova.

❖ An iron with good steam action: an iron is a quilter's best friend and can sort out a multitude of minor problems.

❖ A large pair of sharp scissors for general fabric cutting: tie a length of ribbon or sew a name tape around the handle for clear identification (fabric scissors should not be used on other materials such as paper, as this blunts them).

❖ A pair of small, very sharp scissors for cutting threads and undoing sewing mistakes. Keep them next to the sewing machine or close by when quilting by hand.

❖ All-purpose, 100 per cent cotton sewing thread in neutral colours, such as ecru or taupe, for machine-piecing and hand-sewing binding (I use Gütermann).

❖ Sticky Post-it notes for numbering piles or rows of fabrics.

❖ A box of long, glass-headed quilter's pins and a pincushion.

❖ Masking tape for marking quilting lines when hand-quilting (or chalk or marker pens).

❖ Thread for quilting. This can be 100 per cent cotton quilting cotton (such as Mettler or Gütermann); cotton perlé 5, 8 or 16; six-strand cotton embroidery thread; silk or linen thread; cotton sashiko thread, or any thread you fancy using on your quilt (although note that 100 per cent natural fibres are best).

❖ Needles for hand-quilting: special quilting needles are thin and short – and are too small for me. I prefer to choose a needle that is best suited to the thread and fabric. Generally for cottons this is a fine embroidery needle or sharp, as I like a longer needle, although any slim needle will be fine. More and more, I am using the very long and very sharp sashiko needles for quilting, particularly with thicker threads such as cotton perlé 5 or 8.

❖ A thimble, depending on personal preference. I prefer close-fitting leather thimbles as metal ones fall off my finger all the time, but even these fall off and get lost all the time, so I usually do without.

HOW MUCH FABRIC TO BUY?

I buy all my fabric in the UK by the metre, but I use imperial measurements (yards and inches) when making quilts because my sewing machine has a quarter-inch foot, and all my rulers and mats are set out in inches. If you are buying inspirational fabric by the yard, and do not have a specific project in mind, I would say that it's fine to consider metres and yards interchangeable in this case. But if you are buying for a particular quilt design, please check the exact quantities required before shopping. However, I would urge you to consider buying a fabric that immediately inspires you when you see it, and to buy it in a relatively simple quantity (buy half/one/two metres). If I really, really love something, I buy two metres of it. This may seem extravagant, but as I don't have a very big collection of fabrics (not by some quilters' standards), I don't mind having leftovers that can then be incorporated into another project. I never buy fat quarters of anything ('fat quarters' are pre-cut quarter-yard/metre pieces of fabric, usually 18 x 22in/45.5 x 55cm), because I invariably require more.

 When I started making quilts, I was terrified about making mistakes when cutting and thus wasting fabric. If a design stipulated a frighteningly exact amount, I could guarantee that this would make me so nervous that I would cut the fabric the wrong way and end up with a useless piece. Buying in rounded-up amounts was and continues to be the best way for me to feel comfortable about having sufficient quantities and therefore about making a quilt. I still always buy more than I expect to use; not a great deal more, but always rounding up to the nearest half-metre. (I have learned that there is no such thing as wasted fabric – just fabric waiting its turn.)

 My approach to buying fabrics is far from scientific. I rarely buy all the fabrics for a quilt in one go, as I like to collect the fabrics over a period of time and from different sources. Then I simply get out the fabrics that I have collected and start from there. This may make you nervous if you have never worked this way before, but I assure you that if you relax and let the quilt grow organically according to the fabrics and the way the burgeoning quilt looks, you will soon know when to carry on adding fabrics and when to stop.

 I tend not to plan too far ahead when I begin a quilt and I don't keep to standard bed sizes. Instead, I make my quilts according to the fabrics and time available and let them grow naturally. My quilts may end up wider or longer, narrower or shorter than commercial bedding, but this does not worry me. If you do want to make a quilt to fit a certain size of bed, take some measurements before you begin and calculate your requirements accordingly.

 None of the quilts in this book has been made with a specific bed, room, décor or finished size in mind, but uses can be found. Also, there is nothing to stop you enlarging or reducing any of the quilts simply by increasing or reducing the number of strips or squares or blocks (and therefore the amounts of fabric needed).

MANAGING A FABRIC STASH

Acquiring fabric and building up a personal collection, no matter how modest, is one of the great pleasures of dealing with textiles and making quilts. Even the smallest pile of carefully chosen patterns and colours will catch your eye when you open the cupboard or walk past the shelf, and suggest interesting combinations and narratives. You need only a few fabrics to start playing and sorting: once you have acquired these, you will soon learn how to recognise your own preferences and tastes, and to see what else is needed to extend or complement your collection.

When I first started making quilts, I took the decision not to build a large fabric stash, and I have managed quite happily with a small collection. This is partly because I could see from the outset that it would be all too easy to keep buying fabrics I thought I might possibly like one day but that would in reality stay in the pile forever because I didn't like them quite enough. It would be a lazy rather than a decisive way of buying fabrics, and I knew I would later regret many such purchases. Instead, my collection is actually more of a holding place for fabrics that I know I shall definitely use. Some quilters do have wonderful, enormous stashes that they manage and use cleverly, but you should never be pressurised or deceived into thinking that a huge stash automatically produces lovely quilts. It is the way you use your stash that counts.

As for storage, it pays to look after your fabrics. Keep them flat and neatly folded, out of direct sunlight, and away from heat, odours and anything that might taint or stain them. Although most fabrics are reasonably light-fast, it is annoying to unfold a favourite piece and find that you have sun-bleached fold marks across it.

PREPARING FABRIC

Some quilters do not bother with pre-washing, but I prefer to do this for several reasons. First, there is the risk of dye running. With good-quality quilting fabrics, this rarely happens these days, but I would much rather lose a fabric at the pre-wash stage than have the horror of it running into a finished quilt when I wash it.

Then there is the question of shrinkage (generally calculated to be approximately 2 per cent for quilting cottons). I like to get this out of the way before I begin cutting, rather than sewing up fabrics that could, potentially, shrink at different rates once they are in a quilt.

Also, all new fabrics have 'size' (a very thin layer of gelatinous paste) applied to them before they leave the factory; this adds body and sheen and it is what makes new fabrics feel so crisp and smooth. It comes off in the first wash, leaving a fabric with the slightly softer, more 'used' feel.

Finally, I find that pre-washed fabrics stick together better when it comes to piecing on the sewing machine.

If you decide to pre-wash, do so in a low-temperature, short-cycle wash (maximum 30°C). Take the washed fabrics out and give them a good shake before drying them on a drying rack (not a washing line, as pegging fabrics out can pull them out of shape). As soon as the fabrics are dry, fold and stack them neatly before ironing. If you leave very dry cotton fabrics scrunched up in a pile, it can be incredibly difficult to eradicate the creases when you come to iron them.

Do NOT pre-wash any fragile fabrics such as double gauze, silk, wool, chintz or dry-clean-only fabrics.

CUTTING OUT

You need to know how to use a rotary cutter with a quilter's ruler and a self-healing mat. Although fabrics can be cut out with scissors, a rotary cutter does an infinitely better, far quicker and more accurate job; it produces super-straight, neat edges and allows you to cut through up to four layers of fabric at a time. This is one technique I would recommend that you learn by having someone show you. Alternatively, there are some excellent tutorials online. Remember to always cut away from you and to keep the blade locked at all times when the cutter is not in use.

When making a quilt, begin by cutting out just a few pieces and building up the layout on the floor or design board (see page 148) to see how it is working. If you cut out everything you have, you may feel that you have accomplished something, but you may also find that you don't use it all – the internal dynamics of the quilt will soon tell you what is working and what isn't.

LAYING OUT PIECES

I start by laying out a small part of the quilt. If I am unsure about the way a design will work with the fabrics, I sometimes cut just a few pieces and make a small sample section. Once I am happy with the general design concept, I cut out more pieces as I go along to save on waste and wasteful mistakes. I then lay out the whole thing on the floor (see page 148 for how to deal with lack of space) until every piece is in its place.

Every quilt has a top and a bottom, a right and a wrong way up, so I look at a layout from all angles, often from above (using stepladder, stairs or furniture) to see what is and isn't working. (A reverse magnifying glass can also be helpful in showing up misplacements and fabrics that aren't working.) I leave the layout overnight if possible, because it really helps to see a potential quilt after a period of time before starting to sew it up on the machine. If anyone else is around, I ask them to take a look as well – even if they have no professed design/colour sense, they may see something awkward or clashing.

PIECING

When it comes to piecing quilting cotton fabrics, you do not need to pin or tack the pieces together beforehand. Just feed the fabrics, right sides together and with the edges accurately aligned, under the needle, holding them in place as you sew them. This goes against all the teachings of needlework lessons, I know, but light cottons have enough fibres on the surface to hold the pieces gently together as you feed them under the needle. Occasionally, when sewing two long rows of blocks together, I may pin in a few places to make sure the seams are aligned, and to make it easier to handle the pieces of fabric at the sewing machine.

If you are using slippery silks and wools, or fabrics that move under the needle such as tweed or velvet, it is a good idea to pin pieces together to keep the ends and edges aligned. It's really only by experimenting with pinning (and perhaps even tacking the most difficult fabrics) that you will find out the best ways of handling them.

Like all quilters, I generally use $\frac{1}{4}$in (5mm) seams for all piecing. This may not seem like a lot, but it does work as long as you use cleanly cut fabrics and keep the raw edges of the pieces very carefully aligned as they go under the needle. If you are using fabrics that are prone to fraying, such as silk, tweed or velvet, try to avoid any unnecessary handling so that you don't lose the $\frac{1}{4}$in (5mm) allowance. You may prefer to cut with a $\frac{1}{2}$in (1cm) allowance, but, if you do this, you need to use the same allowance on all the fabrics in the quilt. Alternatively, use a pinking blade on your rotary cutter to reduce fraying.

With light fabrics (for example, cotton or silk), there is no need to do any reverse stitching at the beginning or end of a seam – just cut the loose threads leaving a 1–2in (2.5–5cm) tail – because each seam is later sewn over and will be secured when the piece is sewn to its neighbours. However, with heavier fabrics that fray and come apart easily (such as velvet, tweed or needlepoint), it is worth making a few reverse stitches at the beginning and end of every section of stitching to prevent threads coming loose.

When you are piecing quilt tops with long seams, it is very important that you alternate the direction in which you sew; if you sew long seams from, say, top to bottom every time, there is a danger of the quilt's top square or rectangle ending up more like a parallelogram. You need to start at one end and then begin the next seam at the opposite end in order to balance the tension of the stitching. (Think of it as making a U-turn at the end of a road.) I use a pin each time to mark the end I need to start from next as it is amazing how quickly you can forget.

Once you become used to handling cotton fabrics, you will discover that they have quite a degree of 'give' or stretch. This is very useful when, for example, you find that seams are not matching perfectly, as it is possible to do a little pulling to get sides to match. When doing this during sewing, keep the needle down and gently manipulate the top or bottom fabric as necessary. Or pull gently, pin and then sew. If you are using fabrics without any give (such as ticking or silk), you need to make sure your cutting and piecing is accurate to ensure that all your corners and angles meet correctly.

Iron seams as you go along – for example, when you have made a section or block, and before moving on to the next. Some quilters open out every seam; others press seams to one side. I iron to one side nearly all the time; the only exceptions are with the main seams on the backing fabric, which I open out, and when I am working with thicker fabrics, such as wool, which would make a ridge if pressed to one side. (See instructions for individual quilts for more details on this.)

It is important to iron the seams in a certain direction according to how they meet the next row or block. It is preferable not to join seams pressed to the same side, because this adds up to four layers of fabric and can create ridges in the quilt.

My more relaxed approach to quilting means that I don't trim edges of pieces, rows, blocks or even whole quilts after sewing, because I am always nervous that I might cut too much off. If you do find you have a block or row that looks uneven at the edge, all you need to do is sew it to the next block or row with a straight line, and no one will ever see the less-than-perfect edge.

The same applies to the outer edge of the quilt; if you can sew the binding on in as straight a line as possible, it will hide a multitude of previous sins. I do not mind if the finished outer edge is not plumb-straight. If this does bother you, trim the edge with a rotary cutter and ruler (see page 136). But be careful: it is very easy to get carried away with neatening and to over-trim and spoil the balance and design.

BORDERS

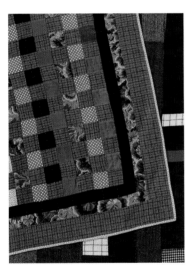

Most of my early quilts did not have borders; I simply took the quilt design right up to the edges. I still like this effect a great deal because it gives density and an old-fashioned feel (lots of vintage quilts don't have borders, probably because there were not enough large pieces of spare fabric available). On the other hand, a border can be invaluable for making a quilt bigger or for framing a design.

Spread the quilt top out on the floor and lay different fabrics next to it in different widths (not cut, just folded or rolled) and see how they work; a border should not be so wide that it swamps the quilt, and not so thin that it is superfluous. A double border can be very useful for framing a quilt (see Warp and Weft, page 114), just as a mount and a frame enhance a photo or painting.

BACKINGS

I am always amazed that we rarely see the backs of quilts in books, yet we see both sides of a quilt when we use it. I think that choosing the backing fabric or fabrics is one of the highlights of making a quilt. It's an opportunity to use a lovely fabric (not just a place to 'hide' bad purchases), and I always feel that the back should offer something of a surprise, something of interest.

I generally don't buy backing fabric until I have finished a quilt top. Sometimes I may get backing fabric in advance because it is good value – but even then it must work well. Other times I have a fabric that I want to use and would rather see it in all its glory and scale on the back than in a drawer. I tend to buy a backing fabric from a shop rather than a website for various reasons: I can fold up the quilt top and take it with me and play with various combinations in the shop, and I don't have to wait for weeks for the fabric to be delivered. At the same time, I can buy the wadding because I now know how large the quilt is; choose the quilting thread, and buy the binding fabric if I don't have enough of a suitable fabric at home.

More and more I am making the backs of my quilts with fabric I already own rather than buying new and fresh fabric. A number of the quilts in this book have backs made up of several fabrics in strips and columns, so that in fact the backs themselves look like modern quilt tops.

WADDING

For me, the decision about wadding is never a problem. I use the same one all the time because it is 100 per cent organic cotton, feels as soft as a baby's bottom, and has 'scrim', which allows you to keep the stitching lines relatively far apart (up to 8in/20cm). I use Hobbs's Heirloom Organic Cotton with scrim, which I used to buy in queen size or king size; however, when I was making the quilts for this book, I discovered that it's possible to buy a huge 96in (245cm)-wide 30yd (27.5m) roll (from Creative Grids; see Resources, page 152). If you know you are going to be making lots of quilts, this is the best and most economical way to buy wadding, and you can use up the off-cuts in smaller quilts. Although you can buy fusible tape to hold pieces of wadding together to make a single piece, I find that this wadding with scrim can be overlapped by a couple of centimetres and it will hold while you make the quilt 'sandwich'. Just make sure you pin the fabric above and under the overlap well so that the layers stay in place while you are quilting. (The 'correct' way is to join the two pieces with large crossover stitches such as mattress stitch.)

Check the fibre content of wadding before buying it; some are 80 per cent cotton and 20 per cent polyester, and have different recommended maximum distances between quilting lines. You should also consider the type of drape you want – the way the quilt folds and hangs. And, of course, you don't have to use wadding; you could use a layer or two of sheeting, or an old blanket or a plain tablecloth.

There is no need to pre-wash wadding, but do check on the packaging to see what the manufacturer recommends and decide what suits you best. Some people iron or hang up wadding before use to get rid of wrinkles and creases, but I just flatten it as I go along.

PUTTING A QUILT TOGETHER AND MAKING THE QUILT SANDWICH

Once you have made the quilt top and the back, the next step is to make a 'quilt sandwich' with the top, the wadding or filling, and the backing. The aim is to make all three layers as smooth as possible ready for quilting then binding.

Lay out the ironed backing fabric (right side down) on the carpet, a bed or on a large table (secure it with bulldog clips). Smooth it out to remove any wrinkles and ridges. The next step is to lay the wadding on top.

Check the packaging for the wadding to find out whether there is a right and wrong side, and whether you need to iron, hang or smooth out the sheet before putting it in the sandwich. Now lay the wadding on top and, working from the centre, smooth it until all wrinkles and creases have been removed. If the wadding is much larger than the backing, trim it with scissors so that both are more or less the same size.

Note that the backing fabric and the wadding should be 3–4in (8–10cm) larger all round than the quilt top.

Next, place the quilt top, right side up, on top of the sandwich layers. Line up any main or central seams to ensure it is sitting correctly and that the outer edges are on the same angles as the outer edges of the back. Make sure it is lying within the framework of the backing and wadding before pinning.

I pin the sandwich together with large glass-headed quilter's pins, pinning every 5–6in (12–15cm) – which takes a lot of pins. I either start from the centre and work out to the sides, or work from one end to the other, constantly smoothing the fabric and adjusting the backing to stop wrinkles forming. Some quilters prefer to use large quilting safety pins, and many also tack the sandwich after pinning. However, I am happy with a pinned quilt, even though it does have to be handled with care.

Just before you pick up the sandwich, trim the excess backing and wadding with scissors if necessary, but do not trim right to the edge of the quilt top as quilts can still move or may need to be slightly adjusted as you quilt. Leave a 3–4in (8–10cm) excess around the edge, which will be cut off after quilting.

QUILTING

My preferred method is to hand-quilt a quilt on my lap without a hoop or frame. This is why and how:

I like the effect of hand-quilting more than that of machine-quilting, but this is a personal preference. I feel it makes a quilt look fuller and less flattened, and gives it an attractive, hand-made appearance.

I like the simplicity of straight lines and the fact that you can see the stitches quite clearly. I use relatively large running stitches, but I sometimes adjust and make shorter stitches if the fabric pieces are smaller.

I use a wadding that allows me to leave quite large spaces between quilting lines (up to 8in/20cm), and this speeds up the stitching process.

For line guidance, I often simply follow the seams of the quilt top, sewing about ¼in (5mm) away from the lines so that I am not trying to get the needle through too many layers of fabric. If I want to create diagonal lines or lines away from seams, I use masking tape to mark a line and stitch along this before pulling it off gently. I don't use any marker pens or stencils.

Even king-sized quilts can be hand-quilted on your lap without a hoop while sitting on a sofa. You simply need to spread out and work methodically from one side or end to the other, smoothing and flattening as you go along.

Hand-quilting is quicker to do than you may think; it's possible to quilt a single-bed-sized quilt in two to four evenings. It also offers the perfect excuse to watch plenty of excellent films.

TYING A QUILT

There are other ways of securing the quilt sandwich. It can of course be machine-quilted, or it can be tied.

Tying is a very simple and quick way of joining the layers of a quilt; it works well with fabrics that are quite thick (such as wool) or that already have surface stitching. Tying is not as durable as hand- or machine-quilting, but has been used successfully for centuries, and has the added benefit of creating interesting points of colour and texture on the top or the back of a quilt. The knots should be tied relatively close together (maximum 6in/15cm apart) or the quilt sandwich will be too loose. Knots look great as close as 2–3in (5–8cm) apart, especially if done in a contrasting colour. It is also worth tying knots at points that follow the design of the quilt, such as in the corners of squares or in the very middle of squares.

Use a cotton perlé thread or all six strands of six-strand cotton embroidery thread. Choose a needle that will go easily through the quilt and thread it with as long a length of cotton as you can manage. Leaving a 2¾in (7cm) loose end on the side of the quilt that will show the knots, make a small stitch in and out at the point to be tied, pulling the thread right through. Without cutting the thread, take the needle to the next tying point and make another little stitch, so that you are making a giant running stitch followed by a tiny running stitch, and so on until you have only enough thread for a 2¾in (7cm) loose end after the last stitch. Cut the thread at the midway point between each stitch, and use the ends to tie a very firm double knot. Trim the ends to the length you prefer.

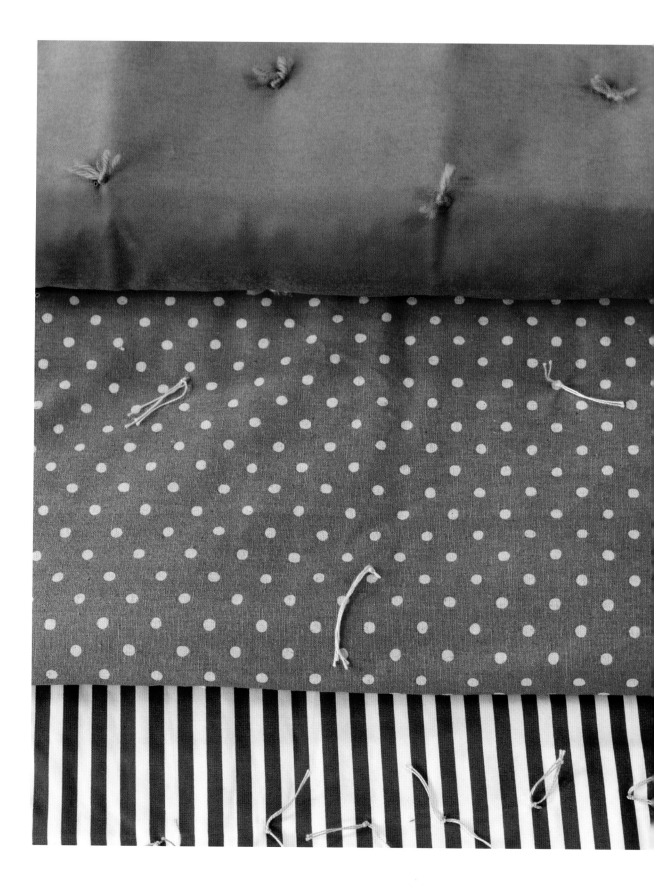

BINDING

Once a quilt has been quilted or tied, trim the excess fabric so that the outer edges of all three layers of the sandwich are aligned. If desired, straighten/trim the edges with a rotary cutter and ruler.

Make a strip of binding that is large enough to go all the way round the quilt, plus approximately 4in (10cm). Cut 2½in (5cm)-wide strips of fabric, either on the straight grain or on the bias. Join enough strips to make one long strip that will fit right around the edge of your quilt.

Cut the ends of the long strip at a 45-degree angle and turn under and press a ¼in (5mm) hem on each end. With wrong sides together, fold the strip in half and press it.

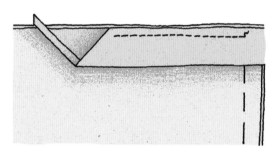

1. On the right side of the quilt and starting a short distance in from the bottom right-hand corner, pin one end of the folded binding strip to the edge of the quilt, with the angled end positioned as shown and the raw edges of the strip aligned with the edge of the quilt. Set the sewing machine to a medium straight stitch and, taking a ¼in (5mm) seam allowance and starting level with the upper folded end, sew the strip to the quilt along one edge. Stop ¼in (5mm) from the end, reverse to secure the threads and then cut them.

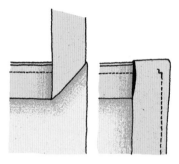

2. Fold the binding over itself, as shown, folding it at a 45-degree angle. Pin the inner edge of the fold to keep it in place. Without distorting the diagonal fold, fold the binding back down so that the raw edges align with the next edge of the quilt. Starting where the last line of machining ended, sew the binding to this edge of the quilt.

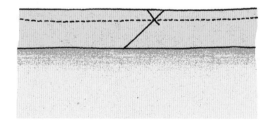

3. Repeat this process at all four corners. When you reach the beginning of the binding strip, tuck the free end inside it and sew over it.

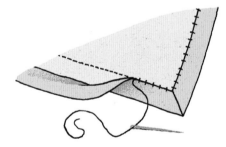

4. Turn the folded edge of the binding over the edge of the quilt and to the back. Arrange it so that it just covers the line of machine stitching and hand-sew it in place. As you reach each corner, mitre it neatly.

FINISHING

Once you have created a lovely quilt, you may want to sew on a personalized label or a label that gives the name of the quilt and the year of making, and/or take a few photographs (especially if you are giving it away).

Now use and enjoy your quilt.

SPACE TO QUILT

Please do not be put off quilting by lack of space. Quilters are renowned for their ingenuity and commitment, and there are many wonderful stories of quilters who have overcome challenges and problems in very overcrowded spaces. Read about the quilters of Gee's Bend if you are in need of inspiration; they will remind you that if you really want to make a quilt, a solution to space problems can always be found.

Much as I would love a room dedicated to quilting, I don't have one. This means that I have had to solve the various problems that many quilters face when making quilts in small, shared spaces. It is possible to work on one strip or row or block at a time, building up the quilt from your seat in front of the sewing machine. If you have the ability to hold designs in your mind while you sew and can visualise how blocks will work together, this at-the-machine approach will work. But if you prefer to lay out the pieces for a whole quilt top before sewing them together, you need to find as much space as possible.

Here are some tips for meeting the challenges of small-space quilting.

Use the biggest floor space available, preferably carpeted (if you lay out fabric pieces on a wooden or tiled floor, they will move in the slightest draught). Bedrooms, living rooms or large hallways are best; you can then use a bed, chair, settee or the stairs as a viewing platform on which to stand and get a good overall view of the quilt.

If necessary, lay out and pick up in one day. This is not ideal, as it really does pay to revisit a quilt a few times and in different lights before you begin to sew it together, even if it means leaving the quilt overnight and looking at it again in the morning. If your time is very limited, you could lay out the pieces, photograph them with a digital camera, and then pick up the pieces in rows, columns or blocks, numbering each one as you go along with sticky notes pinned to the piles. Upload the photos on to the computer, enlarge them and look carefully to see what is working and what is not. If the design needs alterations, you can lay it out again and make changes before putting it back into labelled piles and moving on to the sewing.

Alternatively, lay out the quilt on a large piece of brushed cotton or flannel, spread out on the floor or hung on the wall or on a large design board. The quilt fabric will stick to the flannel, which can be carefully folded or rolled up and brought out again when the carpet, floor or wall space is clear.

If you are really stuck for space, you can use a bed for laying out a quilt. Strip the bed so that you have a flat surface. Alternatively, cover the mattress with a pale, brushed-cotton sheet or large piece of cotton flannel; the quilt pieces will stick to the sheet/flannel, which can then be folded carefully and stored to be brought out when required.

A bed is also a good place for making the sandwich (see page 143). Pin the edges of the backing fabric, right side down, to the mattress, place the wadding or filling on top and then the quilt top (right side up).

A design board can be the best solution to lack of floor space if you are using mostly light cotton fabric, plus it allows you to stand back and scrutinise your quilt design. The board (or 'wall') should be covered in brushed-cotton or cotton flannel in a neutral colour so that cotton fabric can stick to it. It can be something as simple as a large piece of hardboard propped up against a wall, with a brushed-cotton flannel bed sheet stapled on. Alternatively, there are specialist suppliers that sell ready-made design boards/walls, but they can be very expensive.

FURTHER READING
AND INSPIRATION

INSPIRATION FROM FABRICS

These are some of the books and places I turn to when I want to see what quilters have done and can do with different fabrics:

The book that accompanied the wonderful V&A quilt exhibition in 2010 is a particularly useful resource:
Quilts 1700–2010: Hidden Histories, Untold Stories, ed. Sue Prichard (V&A Publishing, 2010)

If you need ideas for how to make the most of what you have got, the quilts made by the Gee's Bend quilters are a reminder of just what can be done with very little in the way of resources. These two books are huge and beautifully illustrated:
The Quilts of Gee's Bend, John Beardsley, et al (Tinwood Books, 2002)
Gee's Bend: The Architecture of the Quilt, William Arnett, et al (Tinwood Books, 2006)

Two generously illustrated books on American quilts by Patricia Cox:
American Quilt Classics: From the Collection of Patricia Cox (Martingale and Company, 2001)
The Ultimate Log Cabin Quilt Book (Collins & Brown, 2004)

And a book on British quilts:
The Quilters' Guild Collection: Contemporary Quilts, Heritage Inspiration, ed. Bridget Long (David & Charles, 2005)

Mary Mashuta's book is beautiful, and full of inspiration for vintage, feedsack and reproduction 1930s fabrics:
Cotton Candy Quilts (CTT Publishing, 2001)

The following museums have good collections of quilts that may provide inspiration and ideas:

The V&A Museum in London
www.vam.ac.uk

The American Museum in Bath
www.americanmuseum.org

Whitworth Art Gallery in Manchester
www.whitworth.manchester.ac.uk

INSPIRATION FROM DESIGNERS

The work of the following designers is full of inspiration for ways to cut, stitch and play with fabrics, and to piece and create quilts:

Denyse Schmidt makes very modern quilts with clean lines and often plain or simple fabrics. More recently, in her second quilt book, she has written about adapting classic designs to make very contemporary quilts:
Quilts (Chronicle Books, 2005)
Modern Quilts, Traditional Inspiration (Stewart, Tabori and Chang, 2012)

Kaffe Fassett is the person who first inspired me to make quilts, and I am still in awe of his incredible colour sense and creativity. The books he wrote with Liza Prior Lucy never fail to get me excited about fabrics and colour. His quilts are also featured, together with those of many well-known designers, in the annual patchwork and quilting books published by Rowan:
Patchwork (Ebury, 1997)
Passionate Patchwork (Ebury, 2001)
V&A Quilts (Ebury, 2005)

Whenever I look at Japanese patchwork and quilting books, I always wish I could hop on a plane to Tokyo to do some fabric shopping. The quilts and ideas are also fresh and innovative, and now the excellent books by Suzuko Koseki, who is probably the most widely known Japanese designer, have been translated into English:

Patchwork Style (Shambhala Publications, 2009)
Natural Patchwork (Trumpeter Books, 2011)
Playful Patchwork (Creative Publishing, 2011)

RESOURCES

This is my address book of shops and suppliers of fabric and quilting equipment. It is by no means comprehensive, as it contains only the places I buy from and am happy to recommend.

SHOPS AND WEBSITES IN LONDON

London is still an amazing place to buy fabric, especially if you are looking to go beyond lightweight quilting cottons. Many specialist fabric shops are still managing to survive and there is a brilliant mix of traditional shops that have been catering to specific trades for years and years, and new, modern places that have been set up to meet the needs of creative stitchers, quilters, sewers and crafty makers. Although there are still a good number of fabric shops in Soho, there are also plenty more scattered about London. Local markets are also worth investigating for good value and/or one-off fabrics. Unfortunately, there is no up-to-date guide to fabric and craft supply shops, although the annual *Time Out* shopping guide includes details of many good places.

The shops in Soho on Berwick and Broadwick Streets and around tend to charge more per metre, but they do have fantastic ranges and have incredibly helpful and knowledgeable staff.

For a large range of natural and beautiful fabrics including ticking, cord, velvet, gingham, linen, silk and lots of cottons:

The Cloth House
47 Berwick Street
London W1F 8SJ
and
98 Berwick Street
London W1F 0QJ
www.clothhouse.com

The following three shops are part of the same group (**www.thesilksociety.com**) and all sell wonderful silks. The Berwick Street Cloth Shop also has velvets, tweeds, wool checks and many glamorous fabrics:

Broadwick Silks
9–11 Broadwick Street
London W1F 0DB

The Silk Society
44 Berwick Street
London W1F 0DB

The Berwick Street Cloth Shop
14 Berwick Street
London W1F 8SE

Liberty is a fantastic source of inspiration and very smart and expensive fabrics. It has an enormous number of Tana Lawn designs and a great haberdashery section; it sells the Olicana fabrics I used in the Ticking and Toile quilt.

Liberty
Great Marlborough Street
London W1B 5AH
www.liberty.co.uk

John Lewis on Oxford Street is excellent for quilting equipment, general haberdashery, a range of quilting cottons, and a wide range of highly quiltable fabrics such as ginghams, plains, linens and dress cottons. Other John Lewis branches in London and nationwide sell varying selections of fabric and haberdashery.

John Lewis
300 Oxford Street
London W1A 1EX
www.johnlewis.com

Joel & Son Fabrics is a treasure trove of fabrics, stocking everything from shirting to suiting, tartans and plaids, to silks and tweeds. It's enormous, not cheap, but is the most comprehensive non-quilting cotton fabric shop I know.

Joel & Son Fabrics
73-83 Church Street
London NW8 8EU
www.joelandsonfabrics.com

Ray Stitch stocks a small but well-chosen selection of fabrics (mostly quilting cottons), good books and magazines, and quilting supplies.

Ray Stitch
Ray Stitch Haberdashery Shop and Café
99 Essex Road
London N1 2SJ
www.raystitch.co.uk

Our Patterned Hand sells fabrics from all over the world with plenty of plains as well as patterned designs. It's aimed more at sewers and general crafts, but the fabrics are ideal for quilts.

Our Patterned Hand
49 Broadway Market
London E8 4PH
www.ourpatternedhand.co.uk

Tikki is a small place with a large range of quilting cottons, but also has some beautiful organic shot cottons and woven stripes. Finnish owner ('tikki' means 'stitch' in Finnish) and ace quilter Tiina stocks the Finca cotton perlé threads that I use so often for quilting in a huge selection of colours. She also runs courses in the back of the shop. It is very close to Kew Gardens and the famous Maids of Honour café, so a visit could be part of a very enjoyable day out.

Tikki
293 Sandycombe Road
London TW9 3LU
www.tikkilondon.com

Delicate Stitches is part of the same business as the London Bead Company, with which it shares premises opposite Kentish Town Tube station. It stocks the best range of threads I know of, and masses of cotton perlé in various thicknesses and shades.

Delicate Stitches
339 Kentish Town Road
London NW5 2TJ
www.londonbeadco.co.uk

Ian Mankin is the man who made ticking so desirable and fashionable in the 1990s, and he is still the top supplier. There's a shop and a website, and an enormous number of lovely fabrics – not just ticking.

Ian Mankin
271/273 Wandsworth Bridge Road
London SW6 2TX
www.ianmankin.co.uk

SHOPS AND WEBSITES OUTSIDE LONDON

The Eternal Maker is my first choice shop and website for quilting cottons and plain fabrics. It has a huge number of fabrics in a large hangar-like shop; the mail-order side is also excellent, very fast and reliable. This is the best place in the UK for Japanese prints.

The Eternal Maker
41 Terminus Road
Chichester
West Sussex PO19 8TX
www.eternalmaker.com

I also use the Cotton Patch mail-order service for quilting cotton fabrics, quilting equipment and sashiko supplies (needles and threads).

The Cotton Patch
1283–1285 Stratford Road
Hall Green
Birmingham B28 9AJ
www.cottonpatch.co.uk

Fancy Moon (website only) offers a fresh, lively, modern range of mostly quilting cottons that are often not carried by other UK websites.
www.fancymoon.co.uk

For an amazing selection of striped canvas, go to Deckchair Stripes. The company also sells bags of swatches (long strips) and sets of squares specifically for patchwork.
www.deckchairstripes.com

Creative Grids is the place to go for all your quilting equipment: the choice is vast. This is also where to come for mats, cutters, rulers, templates and wadding, in particular the 30yd (27.5m) roll of organic cotton with scrim that works out at such good value per quilt.
www.creativegrids.com

Tinsmiths has some lovely tickings.
www.shop.tinsmiths.co.uk

VINTAGE

Vintage fabrics are highly sought-after these days, and the prices have risen accordingly. This means that it can be very expensive to make a whole quilt with lovely vintage fabrics, but one piece might inspire a design into which other fabrics can be introduced.

eBay is the best source of vintage hand-embroidered textiles; it is also good for other types of vintage fabrics plus Harris tweed and French linens.
www.ebay.co.uk

There are several specialist vintage fabric sellers such as Donna Flower, who has an enviably large collection of fabrics from many decades of the twentieth century.
www.donnaflower.com

Vintage fairs, festivals and markets where independent dealers are selling are all good places to look out for vintage fabric.

SHOPS AND WEBSITES OUTSIDE THE UK

Purl is the shop I wish I could have on my doorstep. It's the place of textile dreams, and even a visit to the website and the blog, Purl Bee, can inspire all sorts of projects. There is the gem of the shop in Manhattan and an excellent website for mail order.

Purl
459 Broome Street
New York
NY 10013
www.purlsoho.com

eQuilter stocks innumerable quilting cottons, and has a brilliantly designed website that allows you to create a pinboard and play with design ideas, and to search by colour. They post worldwide.
www.equilter.com

Glorious Color stocks the largest selection of Kaffe Fassett and Rowan quilting fabrics plus books, bundles and kits, and the service is excellent.
www.gloriouscolor.com

Hawthorne Threads has a lovely selection of fabrics, including all the latest and most sought-after designs and designers. Their delivery service is fantastic.
www.hawthornethreads.com

QUILT DIRECTORY

Big Print (Marimekko fabric)
57 x 81 in (140 x 200cm)

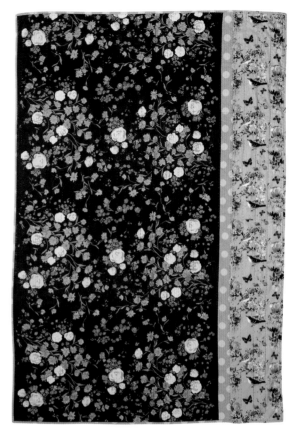

Watercolour
54 x 79in (137 x 200cm)

Quilts shown here
are not to scale.

Scottish Log Cabin
60 x 60in (158 x 158cm)

Needlepoint Squares
44 x 58in (112 x 148cm)

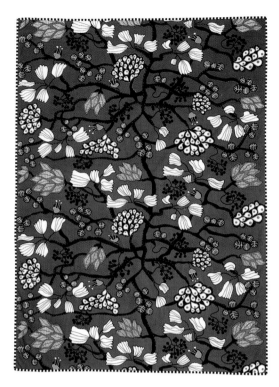

Big Print (IKEA fabric)
58 x 78in (148 x 198cm)

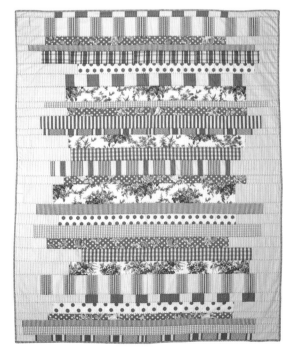

Ticking and Toile
62 x 76in (157.5 x 193cm)

Crinoline Lady
48 x 64in (120 x 160cm)

Granny Takes a Trip
47 x 58½in (119 x 149cm)

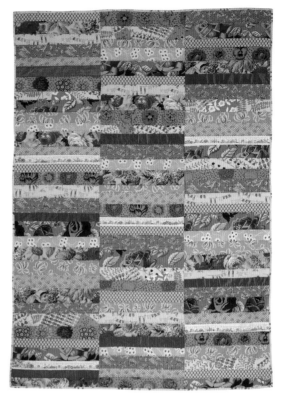

Washing Line
60 x 85in (150 x 216cm)

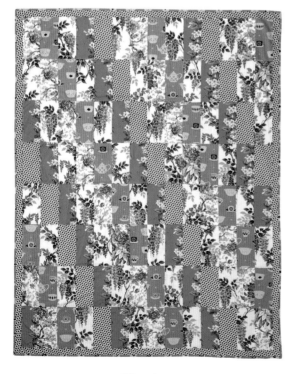

Wisteria
59½ x 79½in (151 x 202cm)

Fall Leaves
56 x 69in (142 x 175.25cm)

Indigo Bento Box
48 x 64in (122 x 162.5cm)

Apples with Apples
56 x 70in (142 x 178cm)

Wardrobe
50 x 61in (127 x 155cm)

Collection
60 x 80in (150 x 200cm)

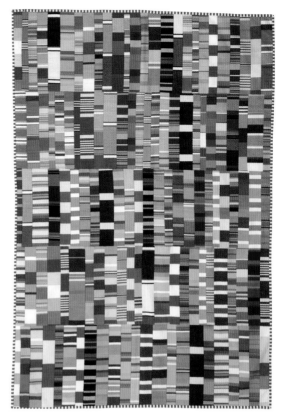

Harlequin
46½ x 62in (118 x 157.5cm)

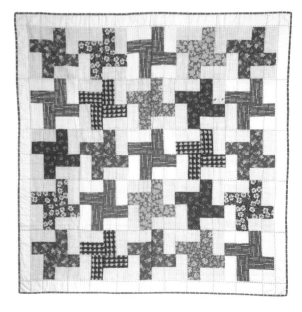

Deckchair Stripes
46 x 66½in (117 x 169cm)

Warp and Weft
58 x 49in (147.5 x 124.5cm)

Kitchen Sink
66½ x 66½in (169 x 169cm)

ACKNOWLEDGEMENTS

I'd like to say thank you to:

Katie Cowan, Amy Christian and Laura Russell at Collins & Brown. I'm enormously grateful to Amy for all her hard work in overseeing the progress of the book, and to Laura for her brilliant styling and design input.

Catherine Gratwicke for her beautiful photographs.

Additional photography by Rachael Smith (page 122) and Martin Norris (flat shots).

Kate Haxell for bringing her excellent checking and editing skills to bear on the words and instructions.

Laura Russell for the wonderful book design, and Louise Leffler for her layout work.

Sam Brewster for the excellent, clear illustrations.

Anna at The Eternal Maker in Chichester for letting us borrow some of her fabrics for the photographs (the address of her marvellous shop is on page 152).

Victoria Lochhead for her textile expertise and her gift of vintage French linens (see the Kitchen Sink quilt, page 94).

Sarah Stringer at Olicana for the box of fabrics that went into the Ticking and Toile quilt.

Jane Graham Maw and Jennifer Christie at Graham Maw Christie for their invaluable help and advice.

Marion Farrell, Angela Burdett, Anna Marie Roos, Anne Burns-Atkinson and Chloë Evans for their friendship and support when I was finishing this book at a difficult time.

Matthew and Kate, for being there.

Tom, Alice and Phoebe, for their suggestions, comments and distractions.

Simon, who makes it all possible.

INDEX